THE TRAGEDIE OF

Macbeth

In the same series

A PLEASANT CONCEITED HISTORIE, CALLED
THE TAMING OF A SHREW

THE TRAGICALL HISTORIE OF HAMLET PRINCE OF DENMARKE

THE CRONICLE HISTORY OF HENRY THE FIFT:
WITH HIS BATTELL FOUGHT AT AGIN COURT IN FRANCE
TOGETHER WITH AUNTIENT PISTOLL

AN EXCELLENT CONCEITED TRAGEDIE OF ROMEO AND JULIET

THE TRAGŒDY OF OTHELLO, THE MOORE OF VENICE

THE TRAGEDIE OF ANTHONIE, AND CLEOPATRA

THE MOST EXCELLENT HISTORIE OF
THE MERCHANT OF VENICE

TWELFE NIGHT, OR WHAT YOU WILL

M. WILLIAM SHAKE-SPEARE: HIS TRUE CHRONICLE HISTORY OF
THE LIFE AND DEATH OF KING LEAR
AND HIS THREE DAUGHTERS

THE TRAGEDIE OF JULIUS CÆSAR

THE TRAGEDY OF KING RICHARD THE THIRD

A MIDSOMMER NIGHTS DREAME

MEASURE, FOR MEASURE

THE TRAGEDIE OF MACBETH

 PRENTICE HALL
HARVESTER WHEATSHEAF

LONDON • NEW YORK • TORONTO • SYDNEY • TOKYO • SINGAPORE •
MADRID • MEXICO CITY • MUNICH

SHAKESPEAREAN ORIGINALS:
FIRST EDITIONS

THE TRAGEDIE OF

Macbeth

EDITED AND INTRODUCED BY
JAMES RIGNEY

SERIES EDITORS
GRAHAM HOLDERNESS AND BRYAN LOUGHREY

PRENTICE HALL

HARVESTER WHEATSHEAF

First published 1996 by
Prentice Hall Europe
Campus 400, Maylands Avenue
Hemel Hempstead
Hertfordshire, HP2 7EZ
A division of
Simon & Schuster International Group

Designed by Geoff Green

Typeset in 11pt Bembo
by Photoprint, Torquay, Devon

Printed and bound in Great Britain by
T.J. Press (Padstow) Ltd., Padstow, Cornwall

Library of Congress Cataloging-in-Publication Data

Shakespeare, William, 1564–1616.
  [Macbeth]
  The tragedie of Macbeth / edited and introduced
by James Rigney.
    p. cm. — (Shakespearean originals—first editions)
  Includes bibliographical references and index.
  ISBN 0–13–355439–2 (pbk.)
    1. Macbeth, King of Scotland, 11th cent.—Drama.
I. Rigney, James. II. Title. III. Series.
PR2750.B23 1995   96–2694
822.3'3—dc20   CIP

British Library Cataloguing in Publication Data

A catalogue record for this book is available from
the British Library
ISBN 0–13–355439–2

1 2 3 4 5   00 99 98 97 96

Contents

General Introduction	1
Introduction	13
Select Bibliography	29
Textual History	31
TEXT: THE TRAGEDIE OF MACBETH	33
Endnotes	105
Appendix: Photographic facsimiles	117

General Introduction

T H I S series puts into circulation single annotated editions of early modern play-texts whose literary and theatrical histories have been overshadowed by editorial practices dominant since the eighteenth century.

The vast majority of Shakespeare's modern readership encounters his works initially through the standard modernised editions of the major publishing houses, whose texts form the basis of innumerable playhouse productions and classroom discussions. While these textualisations vary considerably in terms of approach and detail, the overwhelming impression they foster is not of diversity but uniformity: the same plays are reprinted in virtually identical words, within a ubiquitous, standardised format. Cumulatively, such texts serve to constitute and define a particular model of Shakespeare's work, conjuring up a body of writing which is given and stable, handed down by the author like holy writ. But the canonical status of these received texts is ultimately dependent not upon a divine creator, but upon those editorial mediations (rendered transparent by the discursive authority of the very texts they ostensibly serve) that shape the manner in which Shakespeare's works are produced and reproduced within contemporary culture.

Many modern readers of Shakespeare, lulled by long-established editorial traditions into an implicit confidence in the object of their attention, probably have little idea of what a sixteenth-century printed play-text actually looked like. Confronted with an example, she or he could be forgiven for recoiling before the intimidating display of linguistic and visual strangeness – antique type, non-standardised spelling, archaic orthographic conventions, unfamiliar and irregular speech prefixes, oddly placed stage directions, and

[1]

possibly an absence of Act and scene divisions. 'It looks more like Chaucer than Shakespeare,' observed one student presented with a facsimile of an Elizabethan text, neatly calling attention to the peculiar elisions through which Shakespeare is accepted as modern, while Chaucer is categorised as ancient. A student reading Chaucer in a modern translation knows that the text is a contemporary version, not a historical document. But the modern translations of Shakespeare which almost universally pass as accurate and authentic representations of an original – the standard editions – offer themselves as simultaneously historical document and accessible modern version – like a tidily restored ancient building.

The earliest versions of Shakespeare's works existed in plural and contested forms. Some nineteen of those plays modern scholars now attribute to Shakespeare (together with the non-dramatic verse) appeared in cheap quarto format during his life, their theatrical provenance clearly marked by an emphasis upon the companies who owned and produced the plays rather than the author.[1] Where rival quartos of a play were printed, these could contrast starkly: the second quarto of *The tragicall historie of Hamlet, prince of Denmarke* (1604), for example, is almost double the length of its first quarto (1603) predecessor and renames many of the leading characters. In 1623, Shakespeare's colleagues Heminge and Condell brought out posthumously the prestigious and expensive First Folio, the earliest collected edition of his dramatic works. This included major works, such as *The Tragedy of Macbeth*, *The Tragedie of Anthonie, and Cleopater*, and *The Tempest*, which had never before been published. It also contained versions of those plays, with the exception of *Pericles*, which had earlier appeared in quarto, versions which in some cases differ so markedly from their notional predecessors for them to be regarded not simply as variants of a single work, but as discrete textualisations independently framed within a complex and diversified project of cultural production; perhaps, even, in some senses, as separate plays. In the case of *Hamlet*, for example, the Folio includes some eighty lines which are not to be found in the second quarto, yet omits a fragment of around 230 lines which includes Hamlet's final soliloquy,[2] and far greater differences exist between certain other pairings.

This relatively fluid textual situation continued throughout the seventeenth century. Quartos of individual plays continued to appear sporadically, usually amended reprints of earlier editions, but occasionally introducing new works, such as the first publication of Shakespeare and Fletcher's *The two noble kinsmen* (1634), a play which was perhaps excluded from the Folio on the basis of its collaborative status.[3] The title of another work written in collaboration with Fletcher, *Cardenio*, was entered on the Stationer's Register of 1653, but it appears not to have been published and the play is now lost. The First Folio proved a commercial success and was reprinted in 1632, although again amended in detail. In 1663, a third edition appeared which in its 1664 reprinting assigned to Shakespeare seven plays, never before printed in folio, viz. *Pericles Prince of Tyre; The London prodigall; The history of Thomas Ld Cromwell; Sir John Oldcastle Lord Cobham; The Puritan widow; A Yorkshire tragedy; The tragedy of Locrine*. These attributions, moreover, were accepted uncritically by the 1685 Fourth Folio.

The assumptions underlying seventeenth-century editorial practice, particularly the emphasis that the latest edition corrects and subsumes all earlier editions, is rarely explicitly stated. They are graphically illustrated, though, by the Bodleian Library's decision to sell off as surplus to requirements the copy of the First Folio it had acquired in 1623 as soon as the enlarged 1663 edition came into its possession.[4] Eighteenth-century editors continued to work within this tradition. Rowe set his illustrated critical edition from the 1685 Fourth Folio, introducing further emendations and modernisations. Alexander Pope used Rowe as the basis of his own text, but he 'corrected' this liberally, partly on the basis of variants contained with the twenty-eight quartos he catalogued but more often relying on his own intuitive judgement, maintaining that he was merely 'restoring' Shakespeare to an original purity which had been lost through 'arbitrary Additions, Expunctions, Transpositions of scenes and lines, Confusions of Characters and Persons, wrong application of Speeches, corruptions of innumerable passages'[5] introduced by actors. Although eighteenth-century editors disagreed fiercely over the principles of their task, all of them concurred in finding corruption at every point of textual transmission (and in Capell's case, composition), and sought the restoration of a perceived poetic genius: for Theobald, Warburton, Johnson and Steevens,

'The multiple sources of corruption justified editorial intervention; in principle at least, the edition that had received the most editorial attention, the most recent edition, was the purest because the most purified.'[6]

This conception of the editorial function was decisively challenged in theory and practice by Edmund Malone, who substituted the principles of archaeology for those of evolution. For Malone, there could be only one role for an editor: to determine what Shakespeare himself had written. Those texts which were closest to Shakespeare in time were therefore the only true authority; the accretions from editorial interference in the years which followed the publication of the First Folio and early quartos had to be stripped away to recover the original. Authenticity, that is, was to be based on restoration understood not as improvement but as rediscovery. The methodology thus offered the possibility that the canon of Shakespeare's works could be established decisively, fixed for all time, by reference to objective, historical criteria. Henceforth, the text of Shakespeare was to be regarded, potentially, as monogenous, derived from a single source, rather than polygenous.

Malone's influence has proved decisive to the history of nineteenth- and twentieth-century bibliographic studies. Despite, however, the enormous growth in knowledge concerning the material processes of Elizabethan and Jacobean book production, the pursuit of Shakespeare's original words sanctioned a paradoxical distrust of precisely those early texts which Malone regarded as the touchstone of authenticity. Many assumed that these texts must themselves have been derived from some kind of authorial manuscript, and the possibility that Shakespeare's papers lay hidden somewhere exercised an insidious fascination upon the antiquarian imagination. Libraries were combed, lofts ransacked, and graves plundered, but the manuscripts have proved obstinately elusive, mute testimony to the low estimate an earlier culture had placed upon them once performance and publication had exhausted their commercial value.

Undeterred, scholars attempted to infer from the evidence of the early printed texts the nature of the manuscript which lay behind them. The fact that the various extant versions differed so considerably from each other posed a problem which could only be partially resolved by the designation of some as 'Bad Quartos', and therefore non-Shakespearean; for even the remaining 'authorised' texts varied between themselves enormously, invariably in terms of detail and often in terms of substance. Recourse to the concept of manuscript authenticity could not resolve the difficulty, for such a manuscript simply does not exist.[7] Faced with apparent textual anarchy, editors sought solace in Platonic idealism: each variant was deemed an imperfect copy of a perfect (if unobtainable) paradigm. Once again, the editor's task was to restore a lost original purity, employing compositor study, collation, conflation and emendation.[8]

Compositor study attempts to identify the working practices of the individuals who set the early quartos and the Folio, and thus differentiate the non-Shakespearean interference, stripping the 'veil of print from a text' and thus attempting 'to recover a number of precise details of the underlying manuscript'.[9] Collation, the critical comparison of different states of a text with a view to establishing the perfect condition of a particular copy, provided systematic classification of textual variations which could be regarded as putative corruptions. Emendation allows the editor to select one of the variations thrown up by collation and impose it upon the reading of the selected control text, or where no previous reading appeared satisfactory, to introduce a correction based upon editorial judgement. Conflation is employed to resolve the larger scale divergences between texts, so that, for example, the Folio *Tragedie of Hamlet, Prince of Denmarke* is often employed as the control text for modern editions of the play, but since it 'lacks' entire passages found only in the second quarto, these are often grafted on to the former to create the fullest 'authoritative' text.

The cuts to the Folio *Hamlet* may reflect, however, not a corruption introduced in the process of transmission, but a deliberate alteration to the text authorised by the dramatist himself. In recent years, the proposition that Shakespeare revised his work and that texts might therefore exist in a variety of forms has attracted considerable support. The most publicised debate has centred on the relationship of the Quarto *M. William Shake-speare: his true chronicle historie of the life and death of King Lear and his three daughters* and the Folio *Tragedie of King Lear*.[10] The editors of the recent Oxford Shakespeare have broken new ground by including both texts in their one-volume edition on the grounds that the *Tragedie* represents an authorial revision of the earlier *Historie*, which is sufficiently radical to justify classifying it as a separate play. Wells and Taylor founded their revisionist position upon a recognition of the fact that Shakespeare was primarily a working *dramatist* rather than literary author and that he addressed his play-texts towards a particular audience of theatrical professionals who were expected to flesh out the bare skeleton of the performance script: 'The written text of any such manuscript thus depended upon an unwritten para-text which always accompanied it: an invisible life-support system of stage directions, which Shakespeare could expect his first audience to supply, or which those first readers would expect Shakespeare himself to supply orally.'[11] They are thus more open than many of their predecessors to the possibility that texts reflect their theatrical provenance and therefore that a plurality of authorised texts may exist, at least for certain of the plays.[12] They remain, however, firmly author centred – the invisible life-support system can ultimately always be traced back to the dramatist himself and the plays remain under his parental authority.[13]

What, however, if it were not Shakespeare but the actor Burbage who suggested, or perhaps insisted on, the cuts to *Hamlet*? Would the Folio version of the play become unShakespearean? How would we react if we *knew* that the Clown spoke 'More than is set down' and that his ad libs were recorded? Or that the King's Men sanctioned additions by another dramatist for a Court performance? Or that a particular text recorded not the literary script of a play but its performance script? Of course, in one sense we cannot know these things. But drama, by its very nature, is overdetermined, the product of multiple influences simultaneously operating across a single site of cultural production. Eyewitness accounts of performances of the period suggest something of the provisionality of the scripts Shakespeare provided to his theatrical colleagues:

> After dinner on the 21st of september, at about two o'clock, I went with my companions over the water, and in the thatched playhouse saw the tragedy of the first Emperor Julius with at least fifteen characters very well acted. At the end of the comedy they danced according to their custom with extreme elegance. Two in men's clothes and two in women's gave this performance, in wonderful combination with each other.[14]

This passage offers what can seem a bizarre range of codes; the thatched playhouse, well-acted tragedy, comic aftermath and elegant transvestite dance, hardly correspond to the typology of Shakespearean drama our own culture has appropriated. The Swiss tourist Thomas Platter was in fact fortunate to catch the curious custom of the jig between Caesar and the boy dressed as Caesar's wife, for by 1612 'all Jigs, Rhymes and Dances' after plays had been 'utterly abolished' to prevent 'tumults and outrages whereby His Majesty's Peace is often broke'.[15] Shakespeare, however, is the 'author' of the spectacle Platter witnessed only in an extremely limited sense; in this context the dramatist's surname functions not simply to authenticate a literary masterpiece, but serves as a convenient if misleading shorthand term alluding to the complex material practices of the Elizabethan and Jacobean theatre industry.[16] It is in the latter sense that the term is used in this series.

Modern theoretical perspectives have destabilised the notion of the author as transcendent subject operating outside history and culture. This concept is in any event peculiarly inappropriate when applied to popular drama of the period. It is quite possible that, as Terence Hawkes argues, 'The notion of a single "authoritative" text, immediately expressive of the plenitude of its author's mind and meaning, would have been unfamiliar to Shakespeare, involved as he was in the collaborative enterprise of dramatic production and notoriously unconcerned to preserve in stable form the texts of most of his plays.'[17] The script is, of course, an integral element of drama, but it is by no means the only one. This is obvious in forms of representation, such as film, dependent on technologies which emphasise the role of the *auteur* at the expense of that of the writer. But even in the early modern theatre, dramatic realisation depended not just upon the scriptwriter,[18] but upon actors, entrepreneurs, promptbook keepers, audiences, patrons, etc.; in fact, the entire wide range of professional and institutional interests constituting the theatre industry of the period.

Just as the scriptwriter cannot be privileged over all other influences, nor can any single script. It is becoming clear that within Elizabethan and Jacobean culture, around each 'Shakespeare' play there circulated a wide variety of texts, performing different theatrical functions and adopting different shapes in different contexts of production. Any of these contexts may be of interest to the modern reader. The so-called Bad Quartos, for example, are generally marginalised as piratically published versions based upon the memorial reconstructions of the plays by bit-part actors. But even if the theory of memorial reconstruction is correct (and it is considerably more controversial than is generally recognised[19]), these quarto texts would provide a unique window on to the plays as they were originally performed and open up exciting opportunities for contemporary performance.[20] They form part, that is, of a rich diversity of textual variation which is shrouded by those traditional editorial practices which have sought to impose a single, 'ideal' paradigm.

In this series we have sought to build upon the pioneering work of Wells and Taylor, albeit along quite different lines. They argue, for example, that

> The lost manuscripts of Shakespeare's work are not the fiction of an idealist critic, but particular material objects which happen at a particular time to have existed, and at another particular time to have been lost, or to have ceased to exist. Emendation does not seek to construct an ideal text, but rather to restore certain features of a lost material object (that manuscript) by correcting certain apparent deficiencies in a second material object (this printed text) which purports to be a copy of the first. Most readers will find this procedure reasonable enough.[21]

The important emphasis here is on the relative status of the two forms, manuscript and printed text: the object of which we can have direct knowledge, the printed text, is judged to be corrupt by conjectural reference to the object of which we can by definition have no direct knowledge, the uncorrupted (but non-existent) manuscript. This corresponds to no philosophical materialism we have encountered. The editors of *Shakespearean Originals* reject the claim that it is possible to construct a rehabilitated text reflecting a form approximating Shakespeare's artistic vision.[22] Instead we prefer to embrace the early printed texts as authentic material objects, the concrete forms from which all subsequent editions ultimately derive.

We therefore present within this series particular textualisations of plays which are not necessarily canonical or indeed even written by *William Shakespeare, Gent*, in the traditional sense; but which nevertheless represent important facets of Shakespearean drama. In the same way that we have rejected the underlying principles of traditional editorial practice, we have also approached traditional editorial procedures with extreme caution, preferring to let the texts speak for themselves with a minimum of editorial mediation. We refuse to allow speculative judgements concerning the exact contribution of the various individuals involved in the production of a given text the authority to license alterations to that text, and as a result relegate compositor study and collation[23] to the textual apparatus rather than attempt to incorporate them into the text itself through emendation.

It seems to us that there is in fact no philosophical justification for emendation, which foregrounds the editor at the expense of the text. The distortions introduced by this process are all too readily incorporated into the text as holy writ. Macbeth's famous lines, for example, 'I dare do all that may become a man, / Who dares do more, is none,' on closer inspection turn out to be Rowe's. The Folio reads, 'I dare do all that may become a man, / Who dares no more is none.' There seems to us no pressing reason whatsoever to alter these lines,[24] and we prefer to confine all such editorial speculation to the critical apparatus. The worst form of emendation is conflation. It is now widely recognised that the texts of the *M. William Shake-speare: his true chronicle historie of King Lear and his three daughters* (1608) and *The Tragedie of King Lear* (1623) differ so markedly that they must be considered as two distinct plays and that the composite *King Lear* which is reproduced in every twentieth-century popular edition of the play is a hybrid which grossly distorts both the originals from which it is derived. We believe that the case of *Lear* is a particularly clear example of a general proposition: that *whenever* distinct textualisations are conflated, the result is a hybrid without independent value. It should therefore go without saying that all the texts in this series are based upon single sources.

The most difficult editorial decisions we have had to face concern the modernisation of these texts. In some senses we have embarked upon a project of textual archaeology and the logic of our position points towards facsimile editions. These, however, are already available in specialist libraries, where they are there marginalised by

[9]

those processes of cultural change which have rendered them alien and forbidding. Since we wish to challenge the hegemony of standard editions by circulating the texts within this series as widely as possible, we have aimed at 'diplomatic' rather than facsimile status and have modernised those orthographic and printing conventions (such as long s, positional variants of u and v, i and j, ligatures and contractions) which are no longer current and likely to confuse. We do so, however, with some misgiving, recognising that as a result certain possibilities open to the Elizabethan reader are thereby foreclosed. On the other hand, we make no attempt to standardise such features as speech prefixes and *dramatis personae*, or impose conventions derived from naturalism, such as scene divisions and locations, upon the essentially fluid and non-naturalistic medium of the Elizabethan theatre. In order that our own editorial practice should be as open as possible we provide as an appendix a sample of the original text in photographic facsimile.

GRAHAM HOLDERNESS AND BRYAN LOUGHREY

NOTES AND REFERENCES

1. The title page of the popular *Titus Andronicus*, for example, merely records that it was 'Plaide by the Right Honourable the Earle of Darbie, Earle of Pembrooke, and Earle of Sussex their Servants', and not until 1598 was Shakespeare's name attached to a printed version of one of his plays, *Love's Labour's Lost*.

2. For a stimulating discussion of the relationship between the three texts of *Hamlet*, see Steven Urkowitz, '"Well-sayd olde Mole", Burying Three *Hamlets* in Modern Editions', in Georgianna Ziegler (ed.), *Shakespeare Study Today* (New York: AMS Press, 1986), pp. 37–70.

3. In the year of Shakespeare's death Ben Jonson staked a far higher claim for the status of the playwright, bringing out the first ever collected edition of English dramatic texts, *The Workes of Beniamin Jonson*, a carefully prepared and expensively produced folio volume. The text of his Roman tragedy *Sejanus*, a play originally written with an unknown collaborator, was carefully revised to preserve the purity of authorial input. See Bryan Loughrey and Graham Holderness, 'Shakespearean Features', in Jean Marsden (ed.), *The Appropriation of Shakespeare: Post-Renaissance Reconstructions of the Works and the Myth* (Hemel Hempstead: Harvester Wheatsheaf, 1991), p. 183.

4. F. Madan and G.M.R. Turbutt (eds), *The Original Bodleian Copy of the First Folio of Shakespeare* (Oxford: Oxford University Press, 1905), p. 5.

5. Cited in D. Nicol Smith, *Eighteenth Century Essays* (Oxford: Oxford University Press, 1963), p. 48.

6. Margreta de Grazia, *Shakespeare Verbatim* (Oxford: Oxford University Press, 1991), p. 62. De Grazia provides the fullest and most stimulating account of the important theoretical issues raised by eighteenth-century editorial practice.

7. Unless the Hand D fragment of 'The Booke of Sir Thomas Moore' (British Library Harleian MS 7368) really is that of Shakespeare. See Stanley Wells and Gary Taylor, *William Shakespeare: A Textual Companion* (Oxford: Oxford University Press, 1987), pp. 461–7.

8. See Margreta de Grazia, 'The Essential Shakespeare and the Material Book', *Textual Practice*, vol. 2, no. 1 (Spring 1988).

9. Fredson Bowers, 'Textual Criticism', in O.J. Campbell and E.G. Quinn (eds), *The Reader's Encyclopedia of Shakespeare* (New York: Methuen, 1966), p. 869.

10. See, for example, Gary Taylor and Michael Warren (eds), *The Division of the Kingdoms* (Oxford: Oxford University Press, 1983).

11. Stanley Wells and Gary Taylor, *William Shakespeare: A Textual Companion* (Oxford: Oxford University Press, 1987), p. 2.

12. See, for example, Stanley Wells, 'Plural Shakespeare', *Critical Survey*, vol. 1, no. 1 (Spring 1989).

13. See, for example, *Textual Companion*, p. 69.

14. Thomas Platter, a Swiss physician who visited London in 1599 and recorded his playgoing; cited in *The Reader's Encyclopaedia*, p. 634. For a discussion of this passage see Richard Wilson, *Julius Caesar: A Critical Study* (Harmondsworth: Penguin, 1992), chapter 3.

15. E.K. Chambers, *The Elizabethan Stage* (Oxford: Oxford University Press, 1923), pp. 340–1.

16. The texts of the plays sometimes encode the kind of stage business Platter recorded. The epilogue of *2 Henry IV*, for example, is spoken by a dancer who announces that 'My tongue is weary; when my legs are too, I will bid you good night . . .'

17. Terence Hawkes, *That Shakespeherian Rag* (London: Methuen, 1986), p. 75.

18. For a discussion of Shakespeare's texts as dramatic scripts, see Jonathan Bate, 'Shakespeare's Tragedies as Working Scripts', *Critical Survey*, vol. 3, no. 2 (1991), pp. 118–27.

19. See, for example, Random Cloud [Randall McLeod], 'The Marriage of

Good and Bad Quartos', *Shakespeare Quarterly*, vol. 33, no. 4 (1982), pp. 421–30.

20. See, for example, Bryan Loughrey, 'Q1 in Modern Performance', in Tom Clayton (ed.), *The 'Hamlet' First Published* (Newark: University of Delaware Press, 1992) and Nicholas Shrimpton, 'Shakespeare Performances in London and Stratford-Upon-Avon, 1984–5', *Shakespeare Survey* 39, pp. 193–7.

21. *Textual Companion*, p. 60.

22. The concept of authorial intention, which has generated so much debate amongst critics, remains curiously unexamined within the field of textual studies.

23. Charlton Hinman's Norton Facsimile of *The First Folio of Shakespeare* offers a striking illustration of why this should be so. Hinman set out to reproduce the text of the original First Folio, but his collation of the Folger Library's numerous copies demonstrated that 'every copy of the finished book shows a mixture of early and late states of the text that is peculiar to it alone'. He therefore selected from the various editions those pages he believed represented the printer's final intentions and bound these together to produce something which 'has hitherto been only a theoretical entity, an abstraction: *the* First Folio'. Thus the technology which would have allowed him to produce a literal facsimile in fact is deployed to create an ahistorical composite which differs in substance from every single original upon which it is based. See Charlton Hinman, *The First Folio of Shakespeare* (New York, 1968), pp. xxiii–xxiv.

24. Once the process begins, it becomes impossible to adjudicate between rival conjectural emendations. In this case, for example, Hunter's suggestion that Lady Macbeth should be given the second of these lines seems to us neither more nor less persuasive than Rowe's.

Introduction

M A C B E T H was first printed in 1623 in the collection of Shakespeare's plays brought together by his theatrical colleagues John Heminge and Henry Condell. This edition, known as the First Folio, is thus the sole authority for the text of *Macbeth*. It might be expected that with all editions of the play deriving from the text in the First Folio – a relatively well-printed text with no hopelessly corrupt passages – the editorial history of the play would be relatively straight-forward. This is not, however, the case. The history of the play's performance and in particular the possible role of collaborators in certain scenes of the play have prompted a long history of editorial judgements derived not from textual evidence but from more obviously subjective criteria.

It is possible that *Macbeth* existed in some earlier form as much as twenty-five years prior to the date of its publication. Internal references within the play have led most editors, since the time of Edmond Malone at the end of the eighteenth century, to place the date of composition around 1606. In March of that year Henry Garnet, the Superior of the Jesuit Order in England, was tried for complicity in the 'Gunpowder Plot' to assassinate King James and his Parliament on 5 November 1605. Accused of extensive perjury in his evidence Garnet claimed that he had a right to equivocate in self-defence. This topical reference is generally seen as lying behind the Porter's line on page 54: 'Faith here's an Equivocator, that could sweare in both the Scales against eyther Scale, who committed Treason enough for Gods sake, yet could not equivocate to Heaven'. Allusions in contemporary works to scenes from *Macbeth* in, for example, Thomas Middleton's *The Puritan, or The Widow of*

Wattling Street (1606–7) all place the play in the middle of the first decade of the seventeenth century.[1]

In his 1947 edition of the play J. Dover Wilson suggested that *Macbeth* was written in the closing years of the reign of Queen Elizabeth, in 1601, and this view was supported by Arthur Melville Clark in *Murder Under Trust* in 1982 (who saw the play as a commentary of King James's escape, while still King of Scotland, from the Gowrie Conspiracy). Daniel Amnéus, in *The Mystery of Macbeth* (1983), went further and argued that given James's strong views on rebellion, and his own much vaunted preservation from it, Shakespeare would not have dared to write a play so concerned with that subject. Martin Holmes had earlier suggested that the history of the Thane of Cawdor had originally been enacted in greater detail but then had been cut down to its present, often confusing abbreviated form because of James's sensitivities. In opposition to Amnéus's argument it can also be maintained that *Macbeth* illustrates the triumph of rightful succession over usurpation and that in many of its features – the celebration of Banquo's line (from which King James traced himself), the theme of witchcraft (which was a particular interest of James) and the reference on page 88 to touching to cure scrofula, the so-called King's Evil (a practice reintroduced by James) – the play pays deliberate tribute to King James and therefore, in this form at least, belongs to the period after James's accession to the English throne in 1603. This was also a period when the topicality of all things Scottish might have made Holinshed's story of Macbeth an attractive source of inspiration.

It is likely that *Macbeth* was one of the plays performed at Hampton Court Palace in August 1606 when King Christian of Denmark, King James's brother-in-law, visited England.[2] Given King James's well-known dislike of long plays a shorter version of *Macbeth* may have been presented on this occasion. In dating the play, therefore, we are left with a date range of 1603–6 but also with the possibility that the play may have been reshaped on a number of occasions during that period. F.G. Fleay, for example, suggested five different versions of the work: an original dating from 1604–5, the play recorded in performance at the Globe in 1610, the First Folio version of 1623, a 1673 version distinguished by the incorporation of two songs for the witches, and the adaptation by Sir William Davenant published in 1674. Fleay suggested that the original text was lost in the fire at the Globe Theatre in 1613.[3]

At 2100 lines *Macbeth* is one of the shortest of Shakespeare's plays, and the shortest of the major tragedies – *Hamlet*, *Othello*, *King Lear* and *Antony and Cleopatra*. Unlike these complex dramatic structures with their spacious encompassment of nature or the political world, *Macbeth* is, as A.C. Bradley observed in *Shakespearean Tragedy*, the most vehement and concentrated of Shakespeare's tragedies. The play begins with a clear focus on Macbeth and is effectively free of subplots; minor figures like Donalbain are abandoned without explanation and significant figures like Lady Macbeth are permitted only a single scene in the second half of the play.[4]

Even within this brief structure there are signs that additions and revisions have been made, so that it is impossible to confidently recapture the text as it was originally performed. The first record of the play in performance is that of the physician and astrologer Simon Forman who saw the play at the Globe Theatre in April 1611. Like Thomas Platter's account of *Julius Cæsar* in 1599, Forman's account, while confirming the general accuracy of the Folio text as a representation of the play, also reveals a play significantly different from that which has come down to us today.

In *The Book of playes and Notes thereof per Forman, for Common Policy*, Forman describes four productions of plays he attended. Of *Macbeth* he left the following record:

> In Mackbeth at the glod 1610 the 20 of Aprill [Saturday] ther was to be observed firste howe Mackbeth and Bancko, 2 noble men of Scotland Ridinge thorowe a wod the[r] stode befor them 3 women feiries or Numphes And saluted Mackbeth sayinge of. 3 tyms unto him haille Mackbeth king of Codon for thou shalt be a kinge but shalt beget No kinges &c and then said Bancko What all to macbeth And nothing to me. yes said the nimphes Haille to thee Banko thou shalt beget kinges yet be no kinge And so they departed & cam to the Courte of Scotland to Dunkin king of Scotes and yt was in the dais of Edward the Confessor. And Dunkin bad them both kindly wellcom. And made Mackbeth forth with the Prince of Northumberland. and sent him hom to his own castell and apppointed mackbeth

to provid for him for he wold Sup with him the next dai at night &
did soe. And mackebeth Contrived to kill Dumkin. & and thorowe
the persuasion of his wife did that night Murder the kinge in his own
Castell beinge his guest. And ther were many prodigies seen that
night & the dai before. And when Mack Beth had murdred the kinge
the blod on his handes could not be washed of by Any means. nor
from his wives handes which handled the bloddi daggers in hiding
them By which means they became both moch amazed & Affronted.
the murder being knowen Dunkins 2 sonns fled the on to England
the [other to] Walles to save them selves. they being fled, they were
supposed guilty of the murder of their father which was nothinge
soe. Then was Mackbeth Crowned kinge and then he for feare of
Banko his old Companion that hre should beget kinges but be no
kinge him selfe he contrived the death of Banko and caused him to
be murdred on the way as he Rode. The next night beinge at supper
with his noble men whom he had bid to a feaste to the which also
Banco should have com, he began to speake of Noble Banco and
wish the he wer ther. And as he thus did standing up to derinck a
Carouse to him. the ghoste of banco came and sate down in his
cheier behind him. And he turninge About to sit down Again sawe
the goste of Banco which fronted him so. that he fell into a great
passion of fear & fury. utteringe many wordes about his murder by
which when they hard that Banco was Murdred they Suspected
Mackbet. Then mack dove fled to England to the kinges sonn And
soe they Raised an Army And cam into scotland. and at dunston
Anyse overthrue mackbet. In the meantym whille macdovee Was in
England mackbet slew mackdoves wife & children. and after in the
battelle mackdove slew mackbet.

Observe Also howe mackbetes quen did Rise in the night in her
slepe & walke and talked and confessed all & the docter noted her
wordes.[5]

Forman's account does not mention Hecate or the cauldron scene,
refers to the weird sisters as nymphs (although this may simply be a
misapprehension on Forman's part or the consequence of interchangeable terms), and has Macbeth and Banquo meet the sisters in
a wood rather than a heath and while on horseback (here Forman
may be incorporating an illustration from Shakespeare's source in
Holinshed's *Chronicles*). The features of Forman's account that
differ from the Folio text as it stands have suggested missing scenes
performed in 1610 but lost by the time the play came to be printed

in 1623. For example, Forman's recollection: 'And when Mack Beth had murdred the kinge the blod on his handes could not be washed of by Any means. nor from his wives handes which handled the bloddi daggers in hiding them', has encouraged the theory that a scene in which Macbeth and Lady Macbeth try to wash blood off their hands has not been preserved in print. Similarly, in the version of the play that Forman saw there was a day's interval between the murder of Banquo and the banquet scene: 'The next night beinge at supper with his noble men whom he had bid to a feaste to the which also Banco should have com, he began to speake of Noble Banco and wish the he wer ther.' In a 1961 discussion of this scene Daniel Amnéus concluded that the lines at the beginning of Act 3, Scene 2 on page 65 where, after Macbeth's entrance, Lady Macbeth greets him, 'How now, my Lord, why doe you keepe alone?' and ending with Macbeth's lines:

> Better be with the dead,
> Whom we, to gayne our peace, have sent to peace,
> Then on the torture of the Minde to lye
> In restless extasie.

along with the murderer's report in Scene 4, were once part of another scene since removed from the Folio text.

R.V. Holdsworth, in the course of arguing that an apparent allusion to *Macbeth* in Middleton's *The Puritan* is in fact an allusion to Middleton's own work, suggests that the reference to 'the ghost ith white sheete' cannot refer to Banquo since:

> What we are to imagine, surely, is that Banquo has risen from his ditch and returned to Dunsinane close behind the Murderer, keeping his promise to 'fail not our feast' on which Macbeth has insisted. Dressing the ghost in the white shroud of a corpse would obscure this idea, and if the supposed allusion to *The Puritan* is discounted it is no longer necessary to assume that this was done.[6]

If, however, Amnéus is right about the missing scene then Holdsworth's reading of the text cannot be sustained so confidently. At another point in Act 2, Scene 3 Rosse enters with Macbeth and Lennox from the chamber of the murdered Duncan: the text gives no indication of where he has been, nor does he speak at all in the subsequent scene. Banquo and Lady Macbeth have come on stage in response to the alarm bell, so Rosse may have come on for the same reason; however, they participate in the scene while he appears to be superfluous. In another version of the play he may have had some function subsequently lost. As it is it is possible to appreciate the decision of the eighteenth-century editor Edmund Capell to cut the character from the scene altogether.

Speculation about the structure of *Macbeth* therefore entails speculation about the context of its performance history. Although Simon Forman saw the play at the Globe Theatre there is evidence to suggest that *Macbeth* had been performed in a range of settings.[7] Reference has already been made to the likely presentation of *Macbeth* at Hampton Court during the visit of the King of Denmark in 1606. In the Jacobean court there was a strong tradition of theatrical performance of which court masques are the most obvious and important examples. Such theatrical events not only provided entertainment for the King and his courtiers, they also gave dramatic and iconographic expression to the ideology of the court and commented on issues of national and European politics. Among Shakespeare's plays, for example, *The Tempest* was performed at the marriage festivities of King James's daughter, Princess Elizabeth, in 1613, while *A Midsummer Nights Dream* was possibly performed at the wedding festivities of the Earl of Derby in 1595 and again at the wedding festivities of the Earl of Southampton in 1598. Assuming that a shorter version of *Macbeth*, appropriate to this setting, was performed at court, scenes cut from the play might well have been preserved for reincorporation when the play was next performed in the public theatre.

In his 1947 edition of the play J. Dover Wilson suggested some of the possible cuts and interpolations that may have taken place between a court and a public performance. He believed that the passage about the hanging of traitors on page 82, the 'milk of concord' passage on page 86 and the reference to curing the King's Evil on page 88 were all additions to the original text. More speculative were his suggested cuts. Among the lost scenes he suggested were a scene between Macbeth and Lady Macbeth falling between Act 1, Scene 3 and Act 1, Scene 4; a scene in Act 2 in which

Lady Macbeth is shown attempting to murder Duncan and a subsequent dialogue between her and Macbeth in the same scene; a speech by Banquo after Macbeth has been made King in which he reflects on the witches' prophecies, a scene which explains the presence of the Third Murderer in Act 3, Scene 3; and a scene in which Macduff explains why he has left his wife and children unprotected.[8] Apart from the dubious dramatic value of some of these attempts to resolve the loose ends of Shakespeare's play there is no positive evidence for any of these cuts. Editors have tended to think of the 'original' *Macbeth* as a play of roughly the same length as *King Lear* or *Othello*. There is, however, no need to formulate a lost text of a somehow fuller and more typical Shakespearean tragedy. The Shakespearean original printed here shows a text full of theatrical possibilities and potential. This degree of openness, particularly in so far as it runs contrary to the notions of authoritative completeness after which the editorial tradition strains, has generated an editorial tradition concerned with the integrity of the text and with the presence of inferior hands in the Folio text. Although interpolations are now seen to be rarer than earlier editors thought, suspicion of them still clouds many judgements about the play.

The text of *Macbeth* is relatively well printed and there are comparatively few instances of verbal corruption or compositorial error. The textual problems of the play, so far as these exist, arise from the signs of rehandling that its structure reveals. The discovery that the two songs evoked in Act 3, Scene 5 and Act 4, Scene 1 existed in full in the manuscript of Thomas Middleton's play *The Witch* encouraged disintegration of the First Folio text with Middleton emerging as the principal suspect in cases where editors were reluctant to ascribe a scene to Shakespeare, generally because it was seen as beneath his usual quality of work. Thus Middleton was assigned, at various stages, Act 1, Scene 1; Act 1, Scene 2, the first thirty-seven lines of Act 1, Scene 3; Act 3, Scene 5 and a cluster of lines in Act 4, Scene 1.

Scholars generally agree that *Macbeth* is printed from a prompt-copy: there are numerous and often very full stage-directions, which at one point, for example, appear to have made their way into the dialogue itself. After the discovery of Duncan's murder by Macduff he rouses the castle:

Introduction

Ring the Alarum Bell: Murder and Treason,
Banquo and Donalbaine: Malcolme awake,
Shake off this Downey sleepe, Deaths counterfeit,
And looke on Death it selfe: up, up, and see
The great Doomes Images: Malcolm, Banquo,
As from your Graves rise up, and walke like Sprights,
To countenance this horror. Ring the Bell.
Bell Rings. Enter Lady.[9]

It has been suggested that this second and superfluous command, 'Ring the Bell' (though contributing to a sense of frantic alarm) is in fact the stage-manager's memo for his own use and appears here as one of Macduff's lines in error.

Despite its dramatic superiority and the fact that, as Coleridge noted, it sets forth the themes of the whole play, the opening scene of the play has been seen by critics such as Henry Cunningham in his first Arden edition of 1912 as superfluous and therefore spurious. This very brief scene sets forth one of the principal interpretative problems of the play, the identity of the witches and the weird sisters. Although the stage-direction refers to the three characters of Act 1, Scene 1 as witches, and Edward Thompson has recently listed a number of features of the presentation of the weird sisters which would seem to indicate that contemporary audiences were expected to recognise them as such, they are not referred to by this word either here or at their later appearances in Act 1, Scene 3 or Act 4, Scene 1: throughout the rest of the play they are referred to as the 'weird sisters'.[9] This causes particular confusion in Act 4, Scene 1 when Hecate arrives with 'the other three witches' – are these attendants who are silent throughout, or is it one of them or one of the weird sisters who delivers the line 'By the pricking of my Thumbes'?[10] In 1884 F.G. Fleay suggested that Middleton's addition to the play (if that was what this scene was agreed to be) contaminated Shakespeare's intention towards the weird sisters by limiting their power of destiny: where Shakespeare saw the weird sisters as masters of the witches, Middleton confused the two and was followed in this confusion by Sir William Davenant in his 1674 adaptation.[11]

The differences in spelling between 'weyward' and 'weyard' within the play might be attributable to different practices between the two compositors; designated Compositor A and Compositor B by Charlton Hinman in *The Printing and Proof Reading of the First Folio of Shakespeare* (1963). The former spelling appears to be A's style while B uses the latter spelling which might indicate the manner in which the word was pronounced. Compositor B is unlikely to have improvised a meaningless neologism in place of an established word such as wayward, particularly since he reproduced wayward accurately in Act 3, Scene 5 where Hecate refers to Macbeth in the lines 'all you have done/Hath bene but for a wayward Sonne' (p. 73). Compositor A is generally regarded as the more accurate of the two across the whole First Folio. However, most cruces in *Macbeth* occur in the earlier scenes, which he set, and most mislineation has also been detected here. In the absence of any hard evidence to enable a distinction to be made, emendation has been carried out according to subjective principles governed by matters of taste. The eighteenth-century editor Lewis Theobald resolved the difference between 'weyward' and 'weyard' as 'weird' and subsequent editors have been led by his practice. The spelling of 'weird' in its adjectival usage is not stable throughout the First Folio. Weyward, A's spelling, with the sense of moody or perverse, is an appropriate word for the three sisters.[12] To substitute weird, from the Anglo-Saxon 'wyrd', referring to fate or destiny, suggests a meaning that the text may not support. It has, however, been a meaning enthusiastically adopted by critics.

Shakespeare's source in Holinshed left some ambiguity as to whether the weird sisters were goddesses of destiny or necromancers endued with the powers of prophecy. The literature of the period, as exemplified in Peter Heylin's 1625 account of the Macbeth story, shows how 'fairies', 'witches' and 'weirds' were interchangeable terms. Subsequent definitions that derive from the word 'weird' and its link with fate have the effect of infringing Macbeth's power of action. If the weird sisters not only foresee but decree the future then Macbeth is a victim of malignant fate rather than of any operation of his own will. For Bradley, for example, for whom operation of character is the essential element of Shakespearean tragedy, the witches cannot be any more than clairvoyant. The desire to resolve the ambiguity that the First Folio permits by its refusal to delimit the range of meanings that Holinshed offered, imposes a meaning on these central characters that may not have been what Shakespeare intended.

A number of editors have rejected the 'bleeding captain' scene in Act 1, Scene 2, or, as is the case with the editors of the Clarendon edition in 1881, suggested that it is the work of Middleton. As W.G. Clark and William Aldis Wright observe in that edition:

> We believe that the second scene of the first act was not written by Shakespeare. Making all allowance for corruption of text, the slovenly metre is not like Shakespeare's work, even when he is most careless. The bombastic phraseology of the sergeant is not like Shakespeare's language even when he is most bombastic. . . . We may add that Shakespeare's good sense would hardly have tolerated the absurdity of sending a severely wounded soldier to carry the news of victory.[13]

This same view is put forward by Cunningham in the Arden edition of 1912. There is, however, no textual evidence to support this theory. Instead, as Clark and Wright's comments show, editors who chose to doubt the scene did so on the basis of unreliable aesthetic criteria. In 1946 B.A. Wright pointed out that the scene perpetuates the Senecan tradition of the heroic narrative:

> The scene in *Macbeth* is directly and obviously relevant, serving no wide purpose than that of presenting the events that precede Macbeth's first encounter with the witches, and consequent assumption of the role of tragic hero. Its scope is that of a prologue, and one feels that Shakespeare would have cast it in that conventional form had he not realised the dramatic superiority of starting the play off on the 'blasted heath'.[14]

Even those who have not attempted to deny Shakespeare responsibility for certain scenes and passages have rejected some parts of the play as beneath Shakespeare's dignity: the Porter scene is the *locus classicus* for this tendency. In Act 1, Scene 5 Lady Macbeth declares:

> Come, thick Night,
> And pall thee in the dunnest smoake of Hell,
> That my keene Knife see not the Wound it makes,
> Nor Heaven peepe through the Blanket of the darke,
> To cry, hold, hold.

Introduction

Samuel Johnson objected to the 'meanness' of the word blanket and Coleridge, following from Johnson, substituted the convoluted notion of 'blank height' for blanket. Something similar occurs in lines 5–7 of Act 1, Scene 7 in the handling of Macbeth's lines:

> Heere,
> But heere, upon this Banke and Schoole of time,
> Wee'ld jumpe the life to come.

Editors tended to follow the conjectural emendation of Lewis Theobald and substitute shoal for school, while making jump mean hazard or risk and therefore making the whole passage a seafaring metaphor – Macbeth would risk a dangerous passage through the shoals in order to gain his ambition. A different, and murkier, meaning is implied by the Folio's 'Schoole'. A.P. Reimer has suggested that gambling terminology drawn from the underworld of sixteenth- and seventeenth-century London is meant. Here a 'bank' means a table or bench on which games of chance are played, the stock of money against which a gambler makes his or her stake, or a particular card-game known as *banco fallito*. 'School' had not yet fully emerged as a term for a collection of gamblers or a place where games of chance were played, but it does appear in the extensive literature of the criminal underworld of the time as a place where card-cheats are trained, and by extension, as a term describing the way of life or act of gaming itself.[15] Where 'shoal' turns Macbeth into a daring overreacher, 'school' makes him a desperate and perhaps despicable gambler.

Such instances, as well as revealing the effects of what is now often silent editorial intervention, emphasise the manner in which *Macbeth* is a powerfully theatrical text. This theatricality is found in its brevity, in its stage history, its fluidity of form, and in the history of the editorial treatment of its text. Ninety years ago E. K. Chambers in his edition of the play for the Warwick Shakespeare acknowledged the overwhelmingly theatrical nature of the text; yet this has been seen by many critics as making the text, in Chamber's words elsewhere, 'unsatisfactory'.[16] Nineteenth-century editors cited these signs of theatrical influence as justification for emending the text:

> The numerous corrections (decidedly and unquestionably so) made by the editors of F2 and the numerous other deviations of the text of

F1, show that the original editors performed their duty in a very imperfect manner, and that, therefore, there is just room for a bolder conjectural criticism of this play than perhaps in any other; neither can the variations of F2 from F1 be always accepted as improvements or authoritative determinations of the true text.[17]

while the Clarendon edition of 1869 commented:

Probably it was printed from a transcript of the author's manuscript, which was in great part not copied from the original, but written to dictation. This is confirmed by the fact that several of the most palpable blunders are blunders of the ear not of the eye.[18]

To the extent that *Macbeth* reveals its origins in circumstances where a variety of venues and occasions called for fluid and easily alterable texts and where collaboration with, and revision by, other writers characterised a system of production quite different from the notions of authorship that were to develop and be codified in the eighteenth century, to that extent *Macbeth* challenges the notions of authority that have been invested in the First Folio.

All of Shakespeare's plays that appeared first in some quarto form were gathered into the First Folio and published in 1623. An additional sixteen plays, including *Macbeth*, were printed for the first time in this volume. The 1623 volume was reprinted as the 'Second Folio' of 1632, which in turn served as the basis of the 'Third Folio' of 1663. This was reissued in 1664 and this reissue was reprinted as the 'Fourth Folio' of 1685. In this history it is the relationship between the various quartos and the First Folio that is of particular importance. The editors of the First Folio make a decisive claim for the legitimacy and authority of their work, assuring purchasers that: 'where [before] you were abused with diverse stolne and surreptitious copies, maimed and deformed by the frauds and stealthes of injurious imposters, that exposed them, even those, are now offered to your view cur'd and perfect of their limbes.'[19] Heminge and Condell thus offer to bring an end to the contested transmission of Shakespeare's plays, to pluck them out of their time and enshrine them within the form of their folio production. However various problems remain which editorial pronouncement cannot altogether remove and which affect, in a fundamental way, the experience of a Shakespearean text.

It has been argued by, for example, Grace Ioppolo, from evidence provided by contemporary practice, that Shakespeare was likely to constantly and thoroughly revise his own plays.[20] None the less, within such theories it is Shakespeare who, alone, is responsible for all the revisions that can be identified in his work. Shakespeare is an authoritative reviser, able to expect that because of his status as the most successful playwright of his era and as a shareholder in the most prosperous company in the pre-Restoration theatre, his views would prevail. He remains the mastering intellect behind the texts. The 'original' text of *Macbeth* helps to reveal how compromised that authority actually was.

An edition of *Macbeth* was published in 1673, prompted by the revival of William Davenant's adaptation of the play at the Dorset Garden in 1672–3. This incorporates the full text of the witches' songs given only their titles in Act 3, Scene 5 of the Folio text. W.W. Greg and F.P. Wilson, in their edition of *The Witch* for the Malone Society (1950), speculate that the company that produced the play in 1672–3 were in possession of a stage-copy of *Macbeth*, rather than that they derived the lines from a manuscript of *The Witch*.[21] *Macbeth* was a popular play in the Restoration period. In his *Roscius Anglicanus* (1708), a contemporary record of dramatic productions, John Downes describes the production, which was premiered in 1663–4 and was revived in 1672–3 throughout the late seventeenth century and into the eighteenth, in the following way:

> The Tragedy of Macbeth, alter'd by Sir William Davenant; being drest in all it's Finery, as new Cloath's, new Scenes, Machines, as flyings for the Witches; with all the Singing and Dancing in it: The first Compos'd by Mr. Lock, the other by Mr. Channell and Mr. Joseph Priest; it being all Excellently perform'd, being in the nature of an Opera, it Recompenc'd double the Expence; it proves still a lasting Play.

Davenant's alteration was published in quarto in 1674, probably in response to an unauthorised publication brought out to capitalise on the popularity of the 1673 revival.[22] Although the title-page announces that the text is 'As it's now acted at the Duke's Theatre', Davenant's name does not appear on the title-page, nor had the work been included in the posthumous folio of his works published in 1673. Macbeth was valued for its theatrical rather than its literary merit, and was popular because of its theatrical and spectacular potential: 'being in the nature of an Opera, it Recompenc'd double the Expence; it proves still a lasting Play'.

Eugene Waith's views on alterations and adaptations, where any feature of the play for which we have a 'good textual authority' must be accounted for in a production, advances an argument for theatrical fidelity to the First Folio text.[23] Waith discusses, for example, the case of the exchange between Malcolm and Macduff in Act 4, Scene 3 and notes that in periods when the theatre favoured spectacle this scene was truncated or done away with because it offered no scope for spectacle, while it was equally unacceptable in periods that favoured realism on the stage. Waith suggests that the formal rhetoric of the scene would not only have been acceptable but popular in Shakespeare's time, and that the scene, in its entirety, served to emphasise the moral divisions of the play. Waith's 'ideal production' is one that is faithful to the whole design of the play as that is presented in the First Folio text, which Waith terms ' a highly organised artistic entity'. *Macbeth*, however, is no such thing, rather it is a collection of theatrical possibilities.

In Act 3, Scene 1, for example, Macbeth recapitulates in his soliloquy much of what has taken place in Act 1, Scene 3 thereby providing a means for shortening Act 1, Scene 3 if necessary, removing Banquo's exchange with the witches. Whether the play would be as dramatically effective without that scene is open to question, but what is implied by this possibility, and other cases like the bleeding captain scene, is that *Macbeth* is a play full of scenes that could be cut and roles that could be dropped. The extent of collaboration, revision by a writer other than Shakespeare, excision and insertion is difficult and perhaps impossible to establish. They do, however, need to be admitted into consideration; they were features characteristic of theatrical practice at the time and the text of *Macbeth* is a spectacular example of that theatrical practice in operation. Heminge and Condell may well have regarded a good playhouse copy that preserved or suggested the protean nature of the play as a 'good text'. That, free of attempts to resolve the alleged corruption of the text, is what is offered here.

Introduction

NOTES AND REFERENCES

1. In respect of the evidence provided by Middleton's play see R.V. Holdsworth's *'Macbeth* and *The Puritan'*, *Notes and Queries*, vol. 37 (1990), pp. 204–5 where Holdsworth argues that the apparent allusion to Banquo's ghost in Middleton's play is in fact a reference to Middleton's own work: 'a typical case of his self-cannibalizing methods of composition' (p. 204)

2. This background is explored in H.N. Paul's *The Royal Play of Macbeth*, (New York: Macmillan, 1950).

3. F.G. Fleay, 'Davenant's *Macbeth* and Shakespeare's Witches', *Anglia*, vol. 7 (1884), pp. 128–44; Fleay's view is supported by K.B. Danks in his paper, 'Is F1 *Macbeth* a Reconstructed Text?' *Notes and Queries*, vol. 4 (1957), pp. 516–17. Daniel Amnéus, by contrast, has argued that there were only three versions of the play in existence: Daniel Amnéus, *The Mystery of Macbeth* (Alhambra, Cal.: Primrose Press, 1983).

4. J.M. Nosworthy's *'Macbeth* at the Globe', *The Library*, 5th series, vol. 2 (1947), pp. 108–18 and R.C. Bald, *'Macbeth* and the Short Plays', *Review of English Studies*, vol. 4 (1928), pp. 429–35 each argue that *Macbeth* was only ever a short play.

5. The original of Forman's manuscript is in Bodleian Library, Oxford, MS Ashmole 208; the transcript above is that found in S. Schoenbaum, *William Shakespeare: Records and Images* (London: Scolar Press, 1981), pp. 7–8; on Forman's account see J.M. Nosworthy's 'Macbeth at the Globe', *The Library*, 5th series, vol. 2 (1947), pp. 108–18.

6. Holdsworth, *'Macbeth* and *The Puritan'*, p. 205.

7. R.C. Bald, for example, analysing the various stage-directions in Macbeth that call for tapers and torches, suggested that this indicated that the prompt-book from which the First Folio text was derived recorded a night performance at court or one held indoors at Blackfriars, both of which would differ from a daytime performance at the Globe: R.C. Bald, *'Macbeth* and the Short Plays'.

8. J. Dover Wilson (ed.), *Macbeth* (The New Shakespeare) (Cambridge: Cambridge University Press, 1947), pp. xxi ff.

9. Edward H. Thompson, 'Macbeth, King James and the Witches', *Studii de limbi si literturi moderne* (Timosoara: Timosoara University Press, 1994), pp. 127–41.

10. Richard Flatter suggested in 1959 that the problem was resolved by 'enter', meaning that the characters moved down to the forestage from the back where the cauldron was the focus. See Richard Flatter,

'Hecate, "the Other Three Witches", and Their Songs', *Shakespeare Jahrbuch*, vol. 95 (1959), pp. 225–37.

11. F.G. Fleay, 'Davenant's *Macbeth* and Shakespeare's Witches', *Anglia*, vol. 7 (1884), pp. 128–44.

12. In Mark Feakin's Theatre ADriFT production at the Greenwich Studio in August and September 1995 the weird sisters were described in the programme as 'Wayward Girl, Wayward Woman and Wayward Boy'. In this same production the weird sisters reappear at the end of the play to drag Macbeth's body off to perdition.

13. W.G. Clark and William Aldis Wright (eds), *Macbeth* (Clarendon Shakespeare) (Oxford: Clarendon Press, 1881), pp. ix–x.

14. B.A. Wright, 'The Bleeding Captain Scene in Macbeth', *Review of English Studies*, vol. 22 (1946), pp. 126–31.

15. A.P. Reimer (ed.), *Macbeth* (Challis Shakespeare) (Sydney: Sydney University Press, 1980), p. 119; see also A.P. Reimer, 'The Bank and School of Time', *Sydney Studies in English*, vol. 5 (1979–90, pp. 96–101.

16. E.K. Chambers (ed.), *Macbeth* (The Warwick Shakespeare) (London: Blackie, 1905), pp. 7–8; E.K. Chambers, *William Shakespeare: A Study of Facts and Problems*, 2 vols (Oxford: Clarendon Press, 1930), vol. i, p. 471.

17. John Hunter (ed.), *Macbeth* (London: Longman, 1870), vol. ii, p. 152.

18. W.G. Clark and William Aldis Wright (eds), *Macbeth* (Clarendon Shakespeare) (Oxford: Clarendon Press, 1889), p. v. The theory that the copy of *Macbeth* was made not by transcription but by hearing has prompted some emendations based on mishearing, such as 'quarell' for 'quary' in Act 1, Scene 2.

19. *Mr William Shakespeares Comedies, Histories & Tragedies. Published according to the True Originall Copies* (London: Printed by Isaac Jaggard and Ed. Blount, 1623), sig. A3.

20. Grace Ioppolo, *Revising Shakespeare* (Cambridge, Mass.: Harvard University Press, 1991).

21. Thomas Middeton, *The Witch*, ed. W.W. Greg and F.P. Wilson (Oxford: Malone Society, 1950), p. xi.

22. On the relation of these quartos to the First Folio see Hazleton Spencer's 'D'Avenant's *Macbeth* and Shakespeare's', *Publications of the Modern Language Association of America*, vol. 40, no. 3 (1925), pp. 619–44.

23. Eugene M. Waith, '*Macbeth*: Interpretation versus Adaptation', in C.T. Prouty (ed.), *Shakespeare for an Age and All Time* (Hamden, Conn.: Shoe String Press, 1954).

Select Bibliography

Amnéus, Daniel, 'A Missing Scene in *Macbeth*', *Journal of English and Germanic Philology*, vol. 60, no. 3 (1961), pp. 435–40.

Amnéus, Daniel A. 'The Cawdor Episode in *Macbeth*', *Journal of English and Germanic Philology*, vol. 63 (1964), pp. 185–90.

Bald, R.C., 'Macbeth and the Short Plays', *Review of English Studies*, vol. 4 (1928), pp. 429–31.

Barker, Richard Hindry, *Thomas Middleton* (Westport, Conn.: Greenwood Press, 1974 (1958)).

Bishop, T.G., 'Reconsidering Folio reading in *Macbeth* 5.1', *Shakespeare Quarterly*, vol. 46 (1995), pp. 76–9.

Chambers, E.K., *William Shakespeare: A Study of Facts and Problems*, 2 vols (Oxford: Clarendon Press, 1930).

Cutts, John P., ' "Speak – Demand – We'll Answer" Hecat(e) and "The Other Three Witches" ', *Shakespeare Jahrbuch*, vol. 96 (1960), pp. 173–76.

Danks, K.B., 'Is F1 *Macbeth* a Reconstructed Text?' *Notes and Queries*, vol. 199 (1957), pp. 516–19.

Easting, Robert, 'Johnson's Note on "Aroint thee, witch" ', *Notes and Queries*, vol. 35 (1988), pp. 480–2.

Flatter, Richard, *Shakespeare's Producing Hand: A Study of his Marks of Expression to be Found in the First Folio* (London: William Heinemann, 1948).

Flatter, Richard, 'The Latest Edition of *Macbeth*', *Modern Philology*, vol. 49 (1951), pp. 124–32.

Flatter, Richard, 'Who Wrote the Hecate Scene?', *Shakespeare Jahrbuch*, vol. 93 (1957), pp. 196–210.

Flatter, Richard, 'Hecate, "The Other Three Witches", and Their Songs', *Shakespeare Jahrbuch*, vol. 95 (1959), pp. 225–37.

Fleay, F.G., 'Davenant's *Macbeth* and Shakespeare's Witches', *Anglia*, vol. 7 (1884), pp. 128–44.

Furness, Horace Howard (ed.), *Macbeth* (New Variorum Shakespeare) (Philadelphia: J.B. Lippincott, 1913).

Select Bibliography

Greg, W.W. and F.P. Wilson (eds), *The Witch* by Thomas Middleton (The Malone Society Reprints) (Oxford: Oxford University Press, 1948 (1950)).

Holdsworth, R.V., '*Macbeth* and *The Puritan*', *Notes and Queries*, vol. 37 (1990), pp. 204–5.

Ioppolo, Grace, *Revising Shakespeare* (Cambridge Mass.: Harvard University Press, 1991).

Johnston, Shirley White, 'Samuel Johnson's Macbeth: "Fair is Foul" ', *The Age of Johnson*, vol. 3 (1990), pp. 189–230.

Kliman, Bernice W., 'Thanes in Folio *Macbeth*', *Shakespeare Bulletin*, vol. 9 (1991), pp. 5–8.

Maxwell, James C., 'The punctuation of *Macbeth* I.i 1–2', *Review of English Studies*, vol. 4 (1953), pp. 356–8.

Maxwell, J.C., '*Macbeth* iv.iii 107', *Modern Language Review*, vol. 51 (1956), p. 73.

Nosworthy, J.M., 'The Bleeding Captain Scene in *Macbeth*', *Review of English Studies*, vol. 22 (1946), pp. 126–30.

Nosworthy, J.M., '*Macbeth* at the Globe', *The Library*, vol. 2 (1947), pp. 108–18.

Nosworthy, J.M., 'The Hecate Scenes in *Macbeth*', *Review of English Studies*, vol. 24 (1948), pp. 138–9.

Parsons, Howard, '*Macbeth*: Some Further Conjectures', *Notes and Queries*, vol. 198 (1953), pp. 54–5.

Parsons, Howard, '*Macbeth*: Emendations', *Notes and Queries*, vol. 199 (1954), pp. 331–3.

Reimer, A.P., 'The Bank and School of Time', *Sydney Studies in English*, vol. 5 (1979–90), pp. 96–101.

Schoenbaum, S., *William Shakespeare: Records and Images* (London: Scolar Press, 1981).

Spencer, Hazleton, 'D'Avenant's Macbeth and Shakespeare's', *Publications of the Modern Language Association of America*, vol. 40 (1925), pp. 619–44.

Thompson, Edward H., '*Macbeth*, King James and the Witches', *Studi de Limbi si Literaturi Moderne* (Timisoara: University of Timisoara Press, 1994).

Treglown, Jeremy, 'Shakespeare's Macbeth's: Davenant, Verdi, Stoppard and the Question of the Theatrical Text', *English*, vol. 29 (1980), pp. 95–113.

Waith, Eugene M., '*Macbeth*: Interpretation versus Adaptation', in C.T. Prouty (ed.), *Shakespeare for an Age and All Time* (Hamden, Conn.: Shoe String Press, 1954).

Wilson, F.P., 'Ralph Crane, Scrivener to the King's Players', *The Library*, vol. 7 (1926), pp. 194–215.

Wright, B.A., 'The Bleeding Captain Scene in *Macbeth*', *Review of English Studies*, vol. 22 (1946), pp. 126–31.

Textual History

M A C B E T H was first printed in 1623 in the First Folio collection of Shakespeare's plays. It occupies twenty-one pages in the Tragedies section (pp. 131–51 inclusive) between *Julius Cæsar* and *Hamlet*. The Act and Scene divisions are indicated, but no *Dramatis Personæ* is provided.

Shakespeare's source is Raphael Holinshed's *Chronicles of England, Scotland, and Ireland* (1587, second edition, 1597). Holinshed's work is based, for its Scottish material, on the *Scotorum Historiae* of Hector Boece (1527) in John Bellenden's 1536 translation. This in its turn used material from John Fordun's *Scotichronicon* (*c.* 1384) and Andrew Wyntown's *Orygynale Cronykil of Scotland* (*c.* 1424). Certain contemporary allusions to the Gunpowder Treason and the curing of the 'King's Evil' appear to have been added to Shakespeare's play to appeal to King James I.

Macbeth is the shortest of the tragedies. Many short lines in the Folio text, some textual obscurities, the frequency with which action is reported rather than shown, and the unusual number of brief scenes have led some critics to the belief that the text has been heavily cut, either as the result of censorship, the requirements of court performance or revision. Most modern editors believe that the First Folio text was set from a prompt-book or transcript of a prompt-book. This is the view, for example, of Kenneth Muir in his Arden edition (1951, 1972, 1984), of G.K. Hunter in the New Penguin edition of 1964, David Bevington in the Bantam edition of 1988 and of Stanley Wells and Gary Taylor in the *Textual Companion* to the Oxford edition of *The Complete Works* (1987).

The first record of the play in performance is at Hampton Court Palace in 1606 as part of the celebrations held for the visit to King

James of his brother-in-law King Christian of Denmark, and another explanation for the length of the play may be that it was thought appropriate to keep the play short if it was, in effect, an official entertainment. This was the view of, for example, A.W. Pollard in *The Foundations of Shakespeare's Text* (1923) and R.C. Bald (in the latter's '*Macbeth* and the "Short Plays" ', *Review of English Studies*, vol. 4 (1928), pp. 429–31. W.W. Greg agreed with this view in his *The Shakespeare First Folio: Its Bibliographical and Textual History* (Clarendon Press, 1955), pp. 389–97).

Nearly all editors have agreed that Act 3, Scene 5, and parts of Act 4, Scene 1 are not by Shakespeare (although they are never omitted from the text on this ground). These scenes are generally attributed to Thomas Middleton. What remains in dispute is whether Middleton collaborated with Shakespeare on the play or whether he adapted Shakespeare's play at a later date.

This edition prints the text of *Macbeth* as it stands in the copy of the First Folio found in Cambridge University Library at shelfmark SS.10.6. In the process of preparing this edition I have also consulted Dover Wilson's 1928 facsimile of the First Folio text. The Endnotes record debts to previous editors of the play, most notably Kenneth Muir's Arden edition.

THE TRAGEDIE OF

Macbeth

Actus Primus. Scena Prima.

Thunder and Lightning. Enter three witches.

1. When shall we three meet againe?
In Thunder, Lightning, or in Raine?
2. When the Hurley-burley's done,
When the Battaile's lost, and wonne.
3. That will be ere the set of Sunne.
1. Where the place?
2. Upon the Heath.
3. There to meet with *Macbeth.*
1. I come, *Gray-Malkin.*
All. Padock calls anon: faire is foule, and foule is faire,
Hover through the fogge and filthie ayre.   *Exeunt.*

Scena Secunda.

*Alarum within. Enter King Malcome, Donal-
baine, Lenox, with attendants, meeting
a bleeding Captaine.*

King. What bloody man is that? he can report,
As seemeth by his plight, of the Revolt
The newest state.

Mal. This is the Serjeant,
Who like a good and hardie Souldier fought
'Gainst my Captivitie: Haile brave friend;
Say to the King, the knowledge of the Broyle,
As thou didst leave it.

    Cap. Doubtfull it stood,
As two spent Swimmers, that doe cling together,
And choake their Art: The mercilesse *Macdonwald*
(Worthie to be a Rebell, for to that
The multiplying Villaines of Nature
Doe swarme upon him) from the Westerne Isles
Of Kernes and Gallowgrosses is supply'd,
And Fortune on his damned Quarry smiling,
Shew'd like a Rebells Whore: but all's too weake:
For brave *Macbeth* (well hee deserves that Name)
Disdayning Fortune, with his brandisht Steele,
Which smoak'd with bloody execution
(Like Valours Minion) carv'd out his passage,
Till hee fac'd the Slave:
Which nev'r shooke hands, nor bad farwell to him,
Till he unseam'd him from the Nave toth'Chops,
And fix'd his Head upon our Battlements.

    King. O valiant Cousin, worthy Gentleman.

    Cap. As whence the Sunne 'gins his reflection,
Shipwracking Stormes, and direfull Thunders:
So from that Spring, whence comfort seem'd to come,
Discomfort swells: Marke King of Scotland, marke,
No sooner Justice had, with Valour arm'd,
Compell'd these skipping Kernes to trust their heeles,
But the Norweyan Lord, surveying vantage,
With furbusht Armes, and new supplyes of men,
Began a fresh assault.

    King. Dismay'd not this our Captaines, *Macbeth* and
Banquoh?

    Cap. Yes, as Sparrowes, Eagles;
Or the Hare, the Lyon:
If I say sooth, I must report they were

The Tragedie of Macbeth

As Cannons over-charg'd with double Cracks,
So they doubly redoubled stroakes upon the Foe:
Except they meant to bathe in reeking Wounds,
Or memorize another *Golgotha*.
I cannot tell: but I am faint,
My Gashes cry for helpe.
    King. So well thy words become thee, as thy wounds,
They smack of Honor both: Goe get him Surgeons.

Enter Rosse and Angus.

Who comes here?
    Mal. The worthy *Thane of Rosse.*
    Lenox. What a haste lookes through his eyes?
So should he looke, that seemes to speake things strange.
    Rosse. God save the King.
    King. Whence cam'st thou, worthy *Thane?*
    Rosse. From Fiffe, great King.
Where the Norweyan Banners flowt the Skie,
And fanne our people cold.
Norway himselfe, with terrible numbers,
Assisted by that most disloyall Traytor,
The *Thane* of Cawdor, began a dismall Conflict,
Till that *Bellona's* Bridegroome, lapt in proofe,
Confronted him with selfe-comparisons,
Point against Point, rebellious Arme 'gainst Arme,
Curbing his lavish spirit: and to conclude,
The Victorie fell on us.
    King. Great happinesse.
    Rosse. That now *Sweno*, the Norwayes King,
Craves composition:
Nor would we deigne him buriall of his men,
Till he disbursed, at Saint *Colmes* ynch,
Ten thousand Dollars, to our generall use.
    King. No more that *Thane* of Cawdor shall deceive
Our Bosome interest: Goe pronounce his present death,
And with his former Title greet *Macbeth.*
    Rosse. Ile see it done.

[35]

King. What he has lost, Noble *Macbeth* hath wonne.

Exeunt.

Scena Tertia.

Thunder. Enter the three Witches.

1. Where hast thou beene, Sister?
2. Killing Swine.
3. Sister, where thou?
1. A Saylors Wife had Chestnuts in her Lappe,
And mouncht, & mouncht, and mouncht:
Give me, quoth I.
Aroynt thee, Witch, the rumpe-fed Ronyon cryes.
Her Husband's to Aleppo gone, Master o'th'Tiger:
But in a Syve Ile thither sayle,
And like a Rat without a tayle,
Ile doe, Ile doe, and Ile doe.
2. Ile give thee a Winde.
1. Th'art kinde.
3. And I another.
1. I my selfe have all the other,
And the very Ports they blow,
All the Quarters that they know,
I'th'Ship-mans Card.
Ile dreyne him drie as Hay:
Sleepe shall neyther Night nor Day
Hang upon his Pent-house Lid:
He shall live a man forbid:
Wearie sev'nights, nine times nine,
Shall he dwindle, peake and pine:
Though his Barke cannot be lost,
Yet it shall be Tempest-tost.
Looke what I have.
2. Shew me, shew me.
1. Here I have a Pilots Thumbe,
Wrackt, as homeward he did come.   *Drum within.*
3. A Drumme, a Drumme:

Macbeth doth come.

  All. The weyward Sisters, hand in hand,
Posters of the Sea and Land,
Thus doe goe, about, about,
Thrice to thine, and thrice to mine,
And thrice againe, to make up nine.
Peace, the Charme's wound up.

    Enter Macbeth and Banquo.

  Macb. So foule and faire a day I have not seene.
  Banquo. How farre is't call'd to Soris? What are these,
So wither'd, and so wilde in their attyre,
That looke not like th'Inhabitants o'th'Earth,
And yet are on't? Live you, or are you aught
That man may question? you seeme to understand me,
By each at once her choppie finger Laying
Upon her skinnie Lips: you should be Women,
And yet your Beards forbid me to interprete
That you are so.
  Mac. Speake if you can: what are you?
  1. All haile *Macbeth*, haile to thee *Thane* of Glamis.
  2. All haile *Macbeth*, haile to thee *Thane* of Cawdor.
  3. All haile *Macbeth*, that shalt be King hereafter.
  Banq. Good Sir, why doe you start, and seeme to feare
Things that doe sound so faire? i'th'name of truth
Are ye fantasticall, or that indeed
Which outwardly ye shew? My Noble Partner
You greet with present Grace, and great prediction
Of Noble having, and of Royall hope,
That he seemes wrapt withall: to me you speake not.
If you can looke into the Seedes of Time,
And say, which Graine will grow, and which will not,
Speake then to me, who neyther begge, nor feare
Your favours, nor your hate.
  1. Hayle.
  2. Hayle.
  3. Hayle.

[37]

1. Lesser then *Macbeth*, and greater.

2. Not so happy, yet much happyer.

3. Thou shalt get Kings, though thou be none:
So all haile *Macbeth*, and *Banquo*.

1. *Banquo*, and *Macbeth*, all haile.

Macb. Stay you imperfect Speakers, tell me more:
By *Sinells* death, I know I am *Thane* of Glamis,
But how, of Cawdor? the *Thane* of Cawdor lives
A prosperous Gentleman: And to be King,
Stands not within the prospect of beleefe,
No more then to be Cawdor. Say from whence
You owe this strange Intelligence, or why
Upon this blasted Heath you stop our way
With such Prophetique greeting?
Speake, I charge you.   *Witches vanish.*

Banq. The Earth hath bubbles, as the Water ha's,
And these are of them: whither are they vanish'd?

Macb. Into the Ayre: and what seem'd corporall,
Melted, as breath into the Winde.
Would they had stay'd.

Banq. Were such things here, as we doe speake about?
Or have we eaten on the insane Root.
That takes the Reason Prisoner?

Macb. Your Children shall be Kings.

Banq. You shall be King.

Macb. And *Thane* of Cawdor too: went it not so?

Banq. Toth'selfe-same tune, and words: who's here?

Enter Rosse and Angus.

Rosse. The King hath happily receiv'd, *Macbeth*,
The newes of thy successe: and when he reades
Thy personall Venture in the Rebels fight,
His Wonders and his Prayses doe contend,
Which should be thine, or his: silenc'd with that,
In viewing o're the rest o'th'selfe-same day,
He findes thee in stout Norweyan Rankes,
Nothing afeared of what thy selfe didst make

Strange Images of death, as thick as Tale
Can post with post, and every one did beare
Thy prayses in his Kingdomes great defence,
And powr'd them downe before him.

   Ang. Wee are sent,
To give thee from our Royall Master thanks,
Onely to harrold thee into his sight,
Not pay thee.

   Rosse. And for an earnest of a greater Honor,
He bad me, from him, call thee *Thane* of Cawdor:
In which addition, haile most worthy *Thane*,
For it is thine.

   Banq. What, can the Devill speake true?

   Macb. The *Thane* of Cawdor lives:
Why doe you dresse me in borrowed Robes?

   Ang. Who was the *Thane*, lives yet,
But under heavie Judgement beares that Life,
Which he deserves to loose.
Whether he was combin'd with those of Norway,
Or did lyne the Rebell with hidden helpe,
And vantage; or that with both he labour'd
In his Countreyes wracke, I know not:
But Treasons Capitall, confess'd, and prov'd,
Have overthrowne him.

   Macb. Glamys, and *Thane* of Cawdor:
The greatest is behinde. Thankes for your paines.
Doe you not hope your Children shall be Kings,
When those that gave the *Thane* of Cawdor to me,
Promis'd no lesse to them.

   Banq. That trusted home,
Might yet enkindle you unto the Crowne,
Besides the *Thane* of Cawdor. But 'tis strange:
And oftentimes, to winne us to our harme,
The Instruments of Darknesse tell us Truths,
Winne us with honest Trifles, to betray's
In deepest consequence.
Cousins, a word, I pray you.

Macb. Two Truths are told,
As happy Prologues to the swelling Act
Of the Imperiall Theame. I thanke you Gentlemen:
This supernaturall solliciting
Cannot be ill; cannot be good.
If ill? why hath it given me earnest of successe,
Commencing in a Truth? I am *Thane* of Cawdor.
If good? why doe I yeeld to that suggestion,
Whose horrid Image doth unfixe my Heire,
And make my seated Heart knock at my Ribbes,
Against the use of Nature? Present Feares
Are lesse then horrible Imaginings:
My Thought, whose Murther yet is but fantasticall,
Shakes so my single state of Man,
That Function is smother'd in surmise,
And nothing is, but what is not.

    Banq. Looke how our Partner's rapt.

    Macb. If Chance will have me King,
Why Chance may Crowne me,
Without my stirre.

    Banq. New Honors come upon him
Like our strange Garments, cleave not to their mould,
But with the aid of use.

    Macb. Come what come may,
Time, and the Houre, runs through the roughest Day.

    Banq. Worthy *Macbeth*, wee stay upon your ley-
sure.

    Macb. Give me your favour:
My dull Braine was wrought with things forgotten.
Kinde Gentlemen, your paines are registred,
Where every day I turne the Leafe,
To reade them.
Let us toward the King: thinke upon
What hath chanc'd: and at more time,
The *Interim* having weigh'd it, let us speake
Our free Hearts each to other.

    Banq. Very Gladly.

Macb. Till then enough:
Come friends.   *Exeunt.*

Scena Quarta.

*Flourish. Enter King, Lennox, Malcolme,
Donalbaine, and Attendants.*

King. Is execution done on *Cawdor*?
Or not those in Commission yet return'd?
  Mal. My Liege, they are not yet come back.
But I have spoke with one that saw him die:
Who did report, that very frankly hee
Confes'd his Treasons, implor'd your Highnesse Pardon,
And set forth a deepe Repentance:
Nothing in his Life became him,
Like the leaving it. He dy'de,
As one that had beene studied in his death,
To throw away the dearest thing he ow'd,
As 'twere a carelesse Trifle.
  King. There's no Art,
To finde the Mindes construction in the Face:
He was a Gentleman, on whom I built
An absolute Trust.

Enter Macbeth, Banquo, Rosse, and Angus.

O worthyest Cousin,
The sinne of my Ingratitude even now
Was heavie on me. Thou art so farre before,
That swiftest Wing of Recompence is slow,
To overtake thee. Would thou hadst lesse deserv'd,
That the proportion both of thanks, and payment,
Might have beene mine: onely I have left to say,
More is thy due, then more then all can pay.
  Macb. The service, and the loyaltie I owe,
In doing it, payes it selfe.
Your Highnesse part, is to receive our Duties:
And our Duties are to your Throne, and State,

Children, and Servants; which doe but what they should,
By doing every thing safe toward your Love
And Honor.

    King. Welcome hither:
I have begun to plant thee, and will labour
To make thee full of growing. Noble *Banquo*,
That hast no lesse deserv'd, nor must be knowne
No lesse to have done so: Let me enfold thee,
And hold thee to my Heart.

    Banq. There if I grow,
The Harvest is your owne.

    King. My plenteous Joyes,
Wanton in fulnesse, seeke to hide themselves
In drops of sorrow. Sonnes, Kinsmen, Thanes,
And you whose places are the nearest, know,
We will establish our Estate upon
Our eldest, *Malcolme*, whom we name hereafter,
The Prince of Cumberland: which Honor must
Not unaccompanied, invest him onely,
But signes of Noblenesse, like Starres, shall shine
On all deservers. From hence to Envernes,
And binde us further to you.

    Macb. The Rest is Labor, which is not us'd for you:
Ile be my selfe the Herbenger, and make joyfull
The hearing of my Wife, with your approach:
So humbly take my leave.

    King. My worthy *Cawdor*.

    Macb. The Prince of Cumberland: that is a step,
On which I must fall downe, or else o're leape,
For in my way it lyes, Starres hide your fires,
Let not Light see my black and deepe desires:
The Eye winke at the Hand; yet let that bee,
Which the Eye feares, when it is done to see.   *Exit*.

    King. True, worthy *Banquo*: he is full so valiant,
And in his commendations, I am fed:
It is a Banquet to me. Let's after him,
Whose care is gone before, to bid us welcome:

It is a peerelesse Kinsman.   *Flourish*   *Exeunt.*

Scena Quinta.

Enter Macbeths Wife alone with a Letter.

Lady. They met me in the day of successe: and I have learn'd
by the perfect'st report, they have more in them, then mortall
knowledge. When I burnt in desire to question them further,
they made themselves Ayre, into which they vanish'd. Whiles
I stood rapt in the wonder of it, came Missives from the King,
who all hail'd me Thane of Cawdor, by which Title before, these
weyward Sisters saluted me, and referr'd me to the comming
on of time, with haile King that shalt be. This have I thought
good to deliver thee (my dearest Partner of Greatnesse) that
thou might'st not loose the dues of rejoycing by being ignorant
of what Greatnesse is promis'd thee. Lay it to thy heart, and
farewell.
Glamys thou art, and Cawdor, and shalt be
What thou art promis'd: yet doe I feare thy Nature,
It is too full o'th'Milke of humane kindnesse,
To catch the neerest way. Thou would'st be great,
Art not without Ambition, but without
The illnesse should attend it. What thou would'st highly,
That would'st thou holily: would'st not play false,
And yet would'st wrongly winne.
Thould'st have, great Glamys, that which cryes,
Thus thou must doe, if thou have it;
And that which rather thou do'st feare to doe,
Then wishest should be undone. High thee hither,
That I may powre my Spirits in thine Eare,
And chastise with the valour of my Tongue
All that impeides thee from the Golden Round,
Which Fate and Metaphysicall ayde doth seeme
To have thee crown'd withall.   *Enter Messenger.*
What is your tidings?
    Mess. The King comes here to Night.
    Lady. Thou'rt mad to say it.

[43]

Is not thy Master with him? who, wer't so,
Would have inform'd for preparation.

   Mess. So please you, it is true: our *Thane* is comming:
One of my fellowes had the speed of him;
Who almost dead for breath, had scarcely more
Then would make up his Message.

   Lady. Give him tending,
He brings great newes.   *Exit Messenger.*
The Raven himselfe is hoarse,
That croakes the fatall entrance of *Duncan*
Under my Battlements. Come you Spirits,
That tend on mortall thoughts, unsex me here,
And fill me from the Crowne to the Toe, top-full
Of direst Crueltie: make thick my blood,
Stop up th'accesse, and passage to Remorse,
That no compunctious visitings of Nature
Shake my fell purpose, nor keepe peace betweene
Th'effect, and hit. Come to my Womans Brests,
And take my Milke for Gall, you murth'ring Ministers,
Where-ever, in your sightlesse substances,
You wait on Natures Mischiefe. Come thick Night.
And pall thee in the dunnest smoake of Hell,
That my keene Knife see not the Wound it makes,
Nor Heaven peepe through the Blanket of the darke,
To cry, hold, hold.   *Enter Macbeth.*
Great Glamys, worthy Cawdor,
Greater then both, by the all-haile hereafter,
Thy Letters have transported me beyond
This ignorant present; and I feele now
The future in the instant.

   Macb. My dearest Love,
Duncan comes here to Night.

   Lady. And when goes hence?

   Macb. To morrow, as he purposes.

   Lady. O never,
Shall Sunne that Morrow see.
Your Face, my *Thane*, is as a Booke, where men

May reade strange matters, to beguile the time.
Looke like the time, beare welcome in your Eye,
Your Hand, your Tongue: looke like th'innocent flower,
But be the Serpent under't. He that's comming,
Must be provided for: and you shall put
This Nights great Businesse into my dispatch,
Which shall to all our Nights, and Dayes to come,
Give solely soveraigne sway, and Masterdome.

   Macb. We will speake further.

   Lady. Onely looke up cleare:
To alter favor, ever is to feare:
Leave all the rest to me.   *Exeunt.*

Scena Sexta.

Hoboyes, and Torches. Enter King, Malcolme,
Donalbaine, Banquo, Lenox, Macduff,
Rosse, Angus, and Attendants.

   King. This Castle hath a pleasant seat,
The ayre nimbly and sweetly recommends it selfe
Unto our gentle sences.

   Banq. This Guest of Summer,
The Temple-haunting Barlet does approve,
By his loved Mansonry, that the Heavens breath
Smells wooingly here: no Jutty frieze.
Buttrice, nor Coigne of Vantage, but this Bird
Hath made his pendant Bed, and procreant Cradle,
Where they must breed, and haunt: I have observ'd
The ayre is delicate.   *Enter Lady.*

   King. See, see, our honor'd Hostesse:
The Love that followes us, sometime is our trouble,
Which still we thanke as Love. Herein I teach you,
How you shall bid God-eyld us for your paines,
And thanke us for your trouble.

   Lady. All our service,
In every point twice done, and then done double,
Were poore, and single Businesse, to contend

[45]

Against those Honors deepe, and broad,
Wherewith your Majestie loades our House:
For those of old, and the late Dignities,
Heap'd up to them, we rest your Ermites.

   King. Where's the *Thane* of Cawdor?
We courst him at the heeles, and had a purpose
To be his Purveyor: But he rides well,
And his great Love (sharpe as his Spurre) hath holp him
To his home before us: Faire and Noble Hostesse
We are your guest to night.

   La. Your Servants ever,
Have theirs, themselves, and what is theirs in compt,
To make their Audit at your Highnesse pleasure,
Still to returne your owne.

   King. Give me your hand:
Conduct me to mine Host we love him highly,
And shall continue, our Graces towards him.
By your leave Hostesse.   *Exeunt.*

Scena Septima.

Ho-boyes.   *Torches.*
Enter a Sewer, and divers Servants with Dishes and Service
over the Stage. Then enter Macbeth.

   Macb. If it were done, when 'tis done, then 'twer well,
It were done quickly: If th'Assassination
Could trammell up the Consequence, and catch
With his surcease, Successe: that but this blow
Might be the be all, and the end all. Heere,
But heere, upon this Banke and Schoole of time,
Wee'ld jumpe the life to come. But in these Cases,
We still have judgement heere, that we but teach
Bloody Instructions, which being taught, returne
To plague th'Inventer This even-handed Justice
Commends th'Ingredience of our poyson'd Challice
To our owne lips. Hee's heere in double trust;
First, as I am his Kinsman, and his Subject,

Strong both against the Deed: Then, as his Host,
Who should against his Murtherer shut the doore,
Not beare the knife my selfe. Besides, this *Duncane*
Hath borne his Faculties so meeke; hath bin
So cleere in his great Office, that his Vertues
Will pleade like Angels, Trumpet-tongu'd against
The deepe damnation of his taking off:
And Pitty, like a naked New-borne-Babe,
Striding the blast, or Heavens Cherubin, hors'd
Upon the sightlesse Curriors of the Ayre,
That teares shall drowne the winde. I have no Spurre
To pricke the sides of my intent, bur onely
Vaulting Ambition, which ore-leapes it selfe,
And falles on th'other.   *Enter Lady.*
How now? What Newes?

   La. He has almost supt: why have you left the chamber?

   Mac. Hath he ask'd for me?

   La. Know you not, he ha's?

   Mac. We will proceed no further in this Businesse:
He hath Honour'd me of late, and I have bought
Golden Opinions from all sorts of people,
Which would be worne now in their newest glosse,
Not cast aside so soone.

   La. Was the hope drunke,
Wherein you drest your selfe? Hath it slept since?
And wakes it now to looke so greene, and pale,
At what it did so freely? From this time,
Such I account thy love. Art thou affear'd
To be the same in thine owne Act, and Valour,
As thou art in desire? Would'st thou have that
Which thou esteem'st the Ornament of Life,
And live a Coward in thine owne Esteeme?
Letting I dare not, wait upon I would,
Like the poore Cat i'th'Addage.

   Macb. Prythee peace:
I dare do all that may become a man,
Who dares no more, is none.

La. What Beast was't then
That made you breake this enterprize to me?
When you durst do it, then you were a man:
And to be more then what you were, you would
Be so much more the man. Nor time, nor place
Did then adhere, and yet you would make both:
They have made themselves, and that their fitnesse now
Do's unmake you. I have given Sucke, and know
How tender 'tis to love the Babe that milkes me,
I would, while it was smyling in my Face,
Have pluckt my Nipple from his Bonelesse Gummes,
And dasht the Braines out, had I so sworne
As you have done to this.

Macb. If we should faile?

Lady. We faile?
But screw your courage to the sticking place,
And wee'le not fayle: when *Duncan* is asleepe,
(Whereto the rather shall his dayes hard Journey
Soundly invite him) his two Chamberlaines
Will I with Wine, and Wassell, so convince,
That Memorie, the Warder of the Braine,
Shall be a Fume, and the Receit of Reason
A Lymbeck onely: when in Swinish sleepe,
Their drenched Natures lyes as in a Death,
What cannot you and I performe upon
Th'unguarded *Duncan*? What not put upon
His spungie Officers? who shall beare the guilt
Of our great quell.

Macb. Bring forth Men-Children onely:
For thy undaunted Mettle should compose
Nothing but Males. Will it not be receiv'd,
When we have mark'd with blood those sleepie two
Of his owne Chamber, and us'd their very Daggers,
That they have don't?

Lady. Who dares receive it other,
As we shall make our Griefes and Clamor rore,
Upon his Death?

Macb. I am settled, and bend up
Each corporall Agent to this terrible Feat.
Away, and mock the time with fairest show,
False Face must hide what the false Heart doth know.

Exeunt.

Actus Secundus. Scena Prima.

*Enter Banquo, and Fleance, with a Torch
before him.*

Banq. How goes the Night, Boy?
Fleance. The Moone is downe: I have not heard the
Clock.
Banq. And she goes downe at Twelve.
Fleance. I take't, 'tis later, Sir.
Banq. Hold, take my Sword:
There's Husbandry in Heaven,
Their Candles are all out: take thee that too.
A heavie Summons lyes like Lead upon me,
And yet I would not sleepe:
Mercifull Powers, restraine in me the cursed thoughts
That Nature gives way to in repose.

Enter Macbeth, and a Servant with a Torch.

Give me my Sword: who's there?
Macb. A Friend.
Banq. What Sir, not yet at rest? the King's a bed.
He hath beene in unusuall Pleasure,
And sent forth great Largesse to your Offices.
This Diamond he greetes your Wife withall,
By the name of most kind Hostesse,
And shut up in measurelesse content.
Mac. Being unprepar'd
Our will became the servant to defect,
Which else should free have wrought.
Banq. All's well.

I dreamt last Night of the three weyward Sisters:
To you they have shew'd some truth.

 Macb. I thinke not of them:
Yet when we can entreat an houre to serve,
We would spend it in some words upon that Businesse,
If you would graunt the time.

 Banq. At your kind'st leysure.

 Macb. If you shall cleave to my consent,
When 'tis, it shall make Honor for you.

 Banq. So I lose none,
In seeking to augment it, but still keepe
My Bosome franchis'd, and Allegeance cleare,
I shall be counsail'd.

 Macb. Good repose the while.

 Banq. Thankes Sir: the like to you.   *Exit Banquo.*

 Macb. Goe bid thy Mistresse, when my drinke is ready,
She strike upon the Bell. Get thee to bed.   *Exit.*
Is this a Dagger, which I see before me,
The Handle toward my Hand? Come, let me clutch thee:
I have thee not, and yet I see thee still.
Art thou not fatall Vision, sensible
To feeling, as to sight? or art thou but
A Dagger of the Minde, a false Creation,
Proceeding from the heat-oppressed Braine?
I see thee yet, in forme as palpable,
As this which now I draw.
Thou marshall'st me the way that I was going,
And such an Instrument I was to use.
Mine Eyes are made the fooles o'th'other Sences,
Or else worth all the rest: I see thee still;
And on thy Blade, the Dudgeon, Gouts of Blood,
Which was not so before. There's no such thing:
It is the bloody Businesse, which informes
Thus to mine Eyes. Now o're the one halfe World
Nature seemes dead, and wicked Dreames abuse
The Curtain'd sleepe: Witchcraft celebrates
Pale *Heccats* Offrings: and wither'd Murther,

Alarum'd by his Centinell, the Wolfe,
Whose howle's his Watch, thus with his stealthy pace,
With *Tarquins* ravishing sides, towards his designe
Moves like a Ghost. Thou sowre and firme-set Earth
Heare not my steps, which they may walke, for feare
Thy very stones prate of my where-about,
And take the present horror from the time,
Which now sutes with it. Whiles I threat, he lives:
Words to the heat of deedes too cold breath gives.

        A Bell rings.

I goe, and it is done: the Bell invites me.
Heare it not, *Duncan*, for it is a Knell,
That summons thee to Heaven, or to Hell. *Exit.*

Scena Secunda.

Enter Lady.

La. That which hath made them drunk, hath made me bold:
What hath quench'd them, hath given me fire.
Hearke, peace: it was the Owle that shriek'd,
The fatall Bell-man, which gives the stern'st good-night.
He is about it, the Doores are open:
And the surfeted Groomes doe mock their charge
With Snores. I have drugg'd their Possets,
That Death and Nature doe contend about them,
Whether they live, or dye.

Enter Macbeth.

Macb. Who's there? what hoa?
Lady. Alack, I am afraid they have awak'd,
And 'tis not done: th'attempt, and not the deed,
Confounds us: hearke: I lay'd their Daggers ready,
He could not misse 'em. Had he not resembled
My Father as he slept, I had don't.
My Husband?
Macb. I have done the deed:

[51]

Didst thou not heare a noyse?

Lady. I heard the Owle schreame, and the Crickets cry.
Did not you speake?

Macb. When?

Lady. Now.

Macb. As I descended?

Lady. I.

Macb. Hearke, who lyes i'th'second Chamber?

Lady. Donalbaine.

Mac. This is a sorry sight.

Lady. A foolish thought, to say a sorry sight.

Macb. There's one did laugh in's sleepe,
And one cry'd Murther, that they did wake each other:
I stood, and heard them: But they did say their Prayers,
And addrest them againe to sleepe.

Lady. There are two lodg'd together.

Macb. One cry'd God blesse us, and Amen the other,
As they had seene me with these Hangmans hands:
Listning their feare, I could not say Amen,
When they did say God blesse us.

Lady. Consider it not so deepely.

Mac. But wherefore could not I pronounce Amen?
I had most need of Blessing, and Amen stuck in my throat.

Lady. These deeds must not be thought
After these wayes: so, it will make us mad.

Macb. Me thought I heard a voyce cry, Sleep no more:
Macbeth does murther Sleepe, the innocent Sleepe,
Sleepe that knits up the ravel'd Sleeve of Care,
The death of each dayes Life, sore Labors Bath,
Balme of hurt Mindes, great Natures second Course,
Chiefe nourisher in Life's Feast.

Lady. What doe you meane?

Macb. Still it cry'd, Sleepe no more to all the House:
Glamis hath murther'd Sleepe, and therefore *Cawdor*
Shall sleepe no more: *Macbeth* shall sleepe no more.

Lady. Who was it, that thus cry'd? why worthy *Thane,*
You doe unbend your Noble strength, to thinke

So braine-sickly of things: Goe get some Water,
And wash this filthie Witnesse from your Hand.
Why did you bring these Daggers from the place?
They must lye there: goe carry them, and smeare
The sleepie Groomes with blood.

  Macb. Ile goe no more:
I am afraid, to thinke what I have done:
Looke on't againe, I dare not.

  Lady. Infirme of purpose:
Give me the Daggers: the sleeping, and the dead,
Are but as Pictures: 'tis the Eye of Child-hood,
That feares a painted Devill. If he doe bleed,
Ile guild the Faces of the Groomes withall,
For it must seeme their Guilt.   *Exit.*
                        Knocke within.

  Macb. Whence is that knocking?
How is't with me, when every noyse appalls me?
What Hands are here? hah: they pluck out mine Eyes.
Will all great *Neptunes* Ocean wash this blood
Cleane from my Hand? no: this my Hand will rather
The multitudinous Seas incarnardine,
Making the Greene one, Red.

                Enter Lady.

  Lady. My Hands are of your colour: but I shame
To weare a Heart so white.   *Knocke.*
I heare a knocking at the South entry:
Retyre we to our Chamber:
A little Water cleares us of this deed.
How easie is it then? your Constancie
Hath left you unattended.   *Knocke.*
Hearke, more knocking
Get on your Night-Gowne, least occasion call us,
And shew us to be Watchers: be not lost
So poorely in your thoughts.

  Macb. To know my deed,   *Knocke.*
'Twere best not know my selfe.

Wake *Duncan* with thy knocking.
I would thou could'st. *Exeunt.*

Scena Tertia.

Enter a Porter.

Knocking within.

Porter. Here's a knocking indeede: if a man were Porter of
Hell Gate, hee should have old turning the Key. *Knock.*
Knock, Knock, Knock. Who's there i'th'name of *Belzebub*?
Here's a Farmer, that hang'd himselfe on th'expectation
of Plentie: Come in time, have Napkins enow about you,
here you'le sweat for't. *Knock.* Knock, knock. Who's
there in th'other Devils Name? Faith here's an Equivocator,
that could sweare in both the Seales against eyther Scale, who
committed Treason enough for Gods sake, yet could not
equivocate to Heaven: oh come in, Equivocator. *Knock.*
Knock, Knock, Knock. Who's there? 'Faith here's an English
Taylor come hither, for stealing out of a French Hose:
Come in Taylor, here you may rost your Goose. *Knock.*
Knock, Knock. Never at quiet: What are you? but this
Place is too cold for Hell. Ile Devill-Porter it no further: I
had thought to have let in some of all Professions, that
goe the Primrose way to th'everlasting Bonfire. *Knock.*
Anon, anon, I pray you remember the Porter.

Enter Macduff, and Lennox.

Macd. Was it so late, friend, ere you went to Bed,
That you doe lye so late?

Port. Faith Sir, we were carowsing till the second Cock:
And Drinke, Sir, is a great provoker of three things.

Macd. What three things does Drinke especially
provoke?

Port. Marry, Sir, Nose-painting, Sleepe, and Urine.
Lecherie, Sir, it provokes, and unprovokes: it provokes
the desire, but it takes away the performance. Therefore
much Drinke may be said to be an Equivocator with Lecherie: it makes him, and it marres him; it sets him on, and it

takes him off; it perswades him, and dis-heartens him; makes him stand too, and not stand too: in conclusion, equivocates him in a sleepe, and giving him the Lye, leaves him.

Macd. I beleeve, Drinke gave thee the Lye last Night.

Port. That it did, Sir, i'the very Throat on me: but I requited him for his Lye, and (I thinke) being too strong for him, though he tooke up my Legges sometime, yet I made a Shift to cast him.

Enter Macbeth.

Macd. Is thy Master stirring?
Our knocking ha's awak'd him: here he comes.

Lennox. Good morrow, Noble Sir.

Macb. Good morrow both.

Macd. Is the *King* stirring, worthy *Thane*?

Macb. Not yet.

Macd. He did command me to call timely on him,
I have almost slipt the houre.

Macb. Ile bring you to him.

Macd. I know this is a joyfull trouble to you:
But yet 'tis one.

Macb. The labour we delight in, Physicks paine:
This is the Doore.

Macd. Ile make so bold to call, for 'tis my limitted
service.   *Exit Macduffe.*

Lenox. Goes the King hence to day?

Macb. He does: he did appoint so.

Lenox. The Night ha's been unruly:
Where we lay, our Chimneys were blowne downe,
And (as they say) lamentings heard i'th'Ayre;
Strange Schreemes of Death,
And Prophecying, with Accents terrible,
Of dyre Combustion, and confus'd Events,
New hatch'd toth' wofull time.
The obscure Bird clamor'd the live-long Night.
Some say, the Earth was fevorous,
And did shake.

Macb. 'Twas a rough Night.
Lenox. My young remembrance cannot paralell
A fellow to it.

Enter Macduff.

Macd. O horror, horror, horror,
Tongue nor Heart cannot conceive, nor name thee.
Macb. and Lenox. What's the matter?
Macd. Confusion now hath made his Master-peece:
Most sacrilegious Murther hath broke ope
The Lords anoynted Temple, and stole thence
The Life o'th'Building.
Macb. What is't you say, the Life?
Lenox. Meane you his Majestie?
Macd. Approch the Chamber, and destroy your sight
With a new *Gorgon*. Doe not bid me speake:
See, and then speake your selves: awake, awake,
                                        Exeunt Macbeth and Lenox.
Ring the Alarum Bell: Murther, and Treason,
Banquo, and *Donalbaine*: *Malcolme* awake,
Shake off this Downey sleepe, Deaths counterfeit,
And looke on Death it selfe: up, up, and see
The great Doomes Image: *Malcolme*, *Banquo*,
As from your Graves rise up, and walke like Sprights,
To countenance this horror. Ring the Bell.

Bell rings. Enter Lady.

Lady. What's the Businesse?
That such a hideous Trumpet calls to parley
The sleepers of the House? speake, speake.
Macd. O gentle Lady,
'Tis not for you to heare what I can speake:
The repetition in a Womans eare,
Would murther as it fell.

Enter Banquo.

O *Banquo*, *Banquo*, Our Royall Master's murther'd.

Lady. Woe, alas:
What, in our House?
    Ban. Too cruell, any where.
Deare *Duff*, I prythee contradict thy selfe,
And say, it is not so.

Enter Macbeth, Lenox, and Rosse.

    Macb. Had I but dy'd an houre before this chance,
I had liv'd a blessed time: for from this instant,
There's nothing serious in Mortalitie:
All is but Toyes: Renowne and Grace is dead,
The Wine of Life is drawne, and the meere Lees
Is left this Vault, to brag of.

Enter Malcolme and Donalbaine.

    Donal. What is amisse?
    Macb. You are, and doe not know't:
The Spring, the Head, the Fountaine of your Blood
Is stopt, the very Source of it is stopt.
    Macd. Your Royall Father's murther'd.
    Mal. Oh, by whom?
    Lenox. Those of his Chamber, as it seem'd, had don't:
Their Hands, and Faces were all badg'd with blood,
So were their Daggers, which unwip'd, we found
Upon their Pillowes: they star'd, and were distracted,
No mans Life was to be trusted with them.
    Macb. O, yet I doe repent me of my furie,
That I did kill them.
    Macd. Wherefore did you so?
    Macb. Who can be wise, amaz'd, temp'rate, & furious,
Loyall, and Neutrall, in a moment? No man:
Th'expedition of my violent Love
Out-run the pawser, Reason. Here lay *Duncan*,
His Silver skinne, lac'd with his Golden Blood,
And his gash'd Stabs, look'd like a Breach in Nature,
For Ruines wastfull entrance: there the Murtherers,
Steep'd in the Colours of their Trade; their Daggers

[57]

Unmannerly breech'd with gore: who could refraine,
That had a heart to love; and in that heart,
Courage, to make's love knowne?

    Lady. Helpe me hence, hoa.

    Macd. Looke to the Lady.

    Mal. Why doe we hold our tongues,
That most may clayme this argument for ours?

    Donal. What should be spoken here,
Where our Fate hid in an augure hole,
May rush, and seize us? Let's away,
Our Teares are not yet brew'd.

    Mal. Nor our strong Sorrow
Upon the foot of Motion.

    Banq. Looke to the Lady:
And when we have our naked Frailties hid,
That suffer in exposure; let us meet,
And question this most bloody piece of worke,
To know it further. Feares and scruples shake us:
In the great Hand of God I stand, and thence,
Against the undivulg'd pretence, I fight
Of Treasonous Mallice.

    Macd. And so doe I.

    All. So all.

    Macb. Let's briefly put on manly readinesse,
And meet i'th'Hall together.

    All. Well contended.   *Exeunt.*

    Malc. What will you doe?
Let's not consort with them:
To shew an unfelt Sorrow, is an Office
Which the false man do's easie.
Ile to England.

    Don. To Ireland, I:
Our seperated fortune shall keepe us both the safer:
Where we are, there's Daggers in mens Smiles;
The neere in blodd, the neerer bloody.

    Malc. This murtherous Shaft that's shot,
Hath not yet lighted: and our safest way,

Is to avoid the ayme. Therefore to Horse,
And let us not be daintie of leave-taking
But shift away: there's warrant in that Theft,
Which steales it selfe, when there's no mercie left.

Exeunt.

Scena Quarta.

Enter Rosse, with an Old man.

Old man. Threescore and ten I can remember well,
Within the Volume of which Time, I have seene
Houres dreadfull, and things strange: but this fore Night
Hath trifled former knowings.
    Rosse. Ha, good Father,
Thou seest the Heavens, as troubled with mans Act,
Threatens his bloody Stage: byth'Clock 'tis Day,
And yet darke Night strangles the travailing Lampe:
Is't Nights predominance, or the Dayes shame,
That Darknesse does the face of earth intombe,
When living Light should kisse it?
    Old man. 'Tis unnaturall,
Even like the deed that's done: On Tuesday last,
A Faulcon towring in her pride of place,
Was by a Mowsing Owle hawkt at, and kill'd.
    Rosse. And *Duncans* Horses,
(A thing most strange, and certaine)
Beauteous, and swift, the Minions of their Race,
Turn'd wilde in nature, broke their stalls, flong out,
Contending 'gainst Obedience, as they would
Make Warre with Mankinde.
    Old man. 'Tis said, they eate each other.
    Rosse. They did so:
To th'amazement of mine eyes that look'd upon't.

Enter Macduffe.

Heere comes the good *Macduffe.*
How goes the world Sir, now?

[59]

Macd. Why see you not?

Ross. Is't known who did this more then bloody deed?

Macd. Those that *Macbeth* hath slaine.

Ross. Alas the day,
What good could they pretend?

Macd. They were subborned,
Malcolme, and *Donalbaine* the Kings two Sonnes
Are stolne away and fled, which puts upon them
Suspition of the deed.

Rosse. 'Gainst Nature still,
Thriftlesse Ambition, that will raven up
Thine owne lives meanes: Then 'tis most like,
The Soveraignty will fall upon *Macbeth*.

Macd. He is already nam'd, and gone to Scone
To be invested.

Rosse. Where is *Duncans* body?

Macd. Carried to Colmekill,
The Sacred Store-house of his Predecessors,
And Guardian of their Bones.

Rosse. Will you to Scone?

Macd. No Cosin, Ile to Fife.

Rosse. Well, I will thither.

Macd. Well may you see things wel done there: Adieu
Least our old Robes fit easier then our new.

Rosse. Farewell, Father.

Old M. Gods benyson go with you, and with those
That would make good of bad, and Friends of Foes.

Exeunt omnes.

Actus Tertius. Scena Prima.

Enter Banquo.

Banq. Thou hast it now, King, Cawdor, Glamis, all,
As the weyward Women promis'd, and I feare
Thou playd'st most fowly for't: yet it was saide
It should not stand in thy Posterity,
But that my selfe should be the Roote, and Father

Of many Kings. If there come truth from them,
As upon thee *Macbeth*, their Speeches shine,
Why by the verities on thee made good,
May they not be my Oracles as well,
And set me up in hope. But hush, no more,

Senit sounded. Enter Macbeth as King, Lady Lenox,
Rosse, Lords, and Attendants.

Macb. Heere's our chiefe Guest.
La. If he had beene forgotten,
It had bene as a gap in our great Feast,
And all-thing unbecomming.
Macb. Tonight we hold a solemne Supper sir,
And Ile request your presence.
Banq. Let your Highnesse
Command upon me, to the which my duties
Are with a most indissoluble tye
For ever knit.
Macb. Ride you this afternoone?
Ban. I, my good Lord.
Macb. We should have else desir'd your good advice.
(Which still hath been both grave, and prosperous)
In this dayes Councell: but wee'le take to morrow.
Is't farre you ride?
Ban. As farre, my Lord, as will fill up the time
'Twixt this, and Supper. Goe not my Horse the better,
I must become a borrower of the Night,
For a darke houre, or twaine.
Macb. Faile not our Feast.
Ban. My Lord, I will not.
Macb. We heare our bloody Cozens are bestow'd
In England, and in Ireland, not confessing
Their cruell Patricide, filling their hearers
With strange invention. But of that to morrow,
When therewithall, we shall have cause of State,
Craving us jointly. Hye you to Horse:
Adieu, till you returne at Night.

Goes *Fleance* with you?

   Ban. I, my good Lord: out time does call upon's.

   Macb. I wish your Horses swift, and sure of foot:
And so doe commend you to their backs.
Farwell.   *Exit Banquo.*
Let every man be master of his time,
Till seven at Night, to make societie
The sweeter welcome:
We will keepe our selfe till Supper time alone:
While then, God be with you.   *Exeunt Lords.*
Sirrha, a word with you: Attend those men
Our pleasure?

   Servant. They are, my Lord, without the Pallace
Gate.

   Macb. Bring them before us.   *Exit Servant.*
To be thus, is nothing, but to be safely thus:
Our feares in *Banquo* sticke deepe,
And in his Royaltie of Nature reignes that
Which would be fear'd. 'Tis much he dares,
And to that dauntlesse temper of his Minde.
He hath a Wisdome, that doth guide his Valour,
To act in safetie. There is none but he,
Whose being I doe feare: and under him,
My *Genius* is rebuk'd, as it is said
Mark Anthonies was by *Caesar.* He chid the Sisters,
When first they put the Name of King upon me,
And bad them speake to him. Then Prophet-like,
They hayl'd him Father to a Line of Kings,
Upon my Head they plac'd a fruitlesse Crowne,
And put a barren Scepter in my Gripe,
Thence to be wrencht with an unlineall Hand,
No Sonne of mine succeeding: if't be so,
For *Banquo's* Issue have I fil'd my Minde,
For them, the gracious *Duncane* have I murther'd,
Put Rancours in the Vessell of my Peace
Onely for them, and mine eternall Jewell
Given to me the common Enemie of Man,

To make them Kings, the Seedes of *Banquo* Kings.
Rather then so, come Fate into the Lyst,
And champion me th'utterance.
Who's there?

Enter Servant, and two Murthers.

Now goe to the Doore, and stay there till we call.

Exit Servant.

Was it not yesterday we spoke together?
    Murth. It was, so please your Highnesse.
    Macb. Well then,
Now have you consider'd of my speeches:
Know, that it was he, in the times past,
Which held you so under fortune,
Which you thought had been our innocent selfe.
This I made good to you, in our last conference,
Past in probation with you:
How you were borne in hand, how crost:
The Instruments: who wrought with them:
And all things else, that might
To halfe a Soule, and to a Notion craz'd,
Say, Thus did *Banquo.*
    1. *Murth.* You made it knowne to us.
    Macb. I did so:
And went further, which is now
Our point of second meeting.
Doe you finde your patience so predominant,
In your nature, that you can let this goe?
Are you so Gospell'd, to pray for this good man,
And for his Issue, whose heavie hand
Hath bow'd you to the Grave, and begger'd
Yours for ever?
    1. *Murth.* We are men, my Liege.
    Macb. I, in the Catalogue ye goe for men,
As Hounds, and Greyhounds, Mungrels, Spaniels, Curres,
Showghes, Water-Rugs, and Demy-Wolves are clipt
All by the Name of Dogges: the valued file

[63]

Distinguishes the swift, the slow, the subtle,
The House-keeper, the Hunter, every one
According to the gift, which bounteous Nature
Hath in him clos'd: whereby he does receive
Particular addition from the Bill,
That writes them all alike: and so of men.
Now, if you have a station in the file,
Not i'th'worst ranke of Manhood, say't,
And I will put that Businesse in your Bosomes,
Whose execution takes your Enemie off,
Grapples you to the heart; and love of us,
Who weare our Health but sickly in his Life,
Which in his Death were perfect.

    2. *Murth.* I am one, my Liege,
Whom the vile Blowes and Buffets of the World
Hath so incens'd, that I am recklesse what I doe,
To spight the World.

    1. *Murth.* And I another,
So wearie with Disasters, tugg'd with Fortune,
That I would set my Life on any Chance,
To mend it or be rid on't.

    Macb. Both of you know *Banquo* was your Enemie.

    Murth. True, my Lord.

    Macb. So is he mine: and in such bloody distance,
That every minute of his being, thrusts
Against my neer'st of Life: and though I could
With bare-fac'd power sweepe him from my sight,
And bid my will avouch it; yet I must not,
For certaine friends that are both his, and mine,
Whose loves I may not drop, but wayle his fall,
Who I my selfe struck downe: and thence it is,
That I to your assistance doe make love,
Masking the Businesse from the common Eye,
For sundry weightie Reasons.

    2. *Murth.* We shall my Lord,
Performe what you command us.

    1. *Murth.* Though our lives——

Macb. Your spirits shine through you,
Within this houre, at most,
I will advise you where to plant your selves,
Acquaint you with the perfect Spy o'th'time,
The moment on't. for't must be done to Night,
And something from the Pallace: always thought,
That I require a clearenesse; and with him,
To leave no Rubs nor Botches in the Worke:
Fleans, his Sonne, that keepes him companie,
Whose absence is no lesse materiall to me,
Then is his Fathers, must embrace the fate
Of that darke houre: resolve your selves apart,
Ile come to you anon.
   Murth. We are resolv'd, my Lord.
   Macb. Ile call upon you straight: abide within,
It is concluded: *Banquo*, thy Soules flight,
If it finde Heaven, must finde it out to Night.   *Exeunt.*

Scena Secunda.

Enter Macbeths Lady, and a Servant.

   Lady. Is *Banquo* gone from Court?
   Servant. I, Madame, but returnes againe to Night.
   Lady. Say to the King, I would attend his leysure,
For a few words.
   Servant. Madame I will.   *Exit.*
   Lady. Nought's had, all's spent,
Where our desire is got without content:
'Tis safer, to be that which we destroy,
Then by destruction dwell in doubtfull joy.

Enter Macbeth.

How now, my Lord, why doe you keepe alone?
Of sorryest Fancies your Companions making,
Using those Thoughts, which should indeed have dy'd
With them they thinke on: things without all remedie
Should be without regard: what's done, is done.
   Macb. We have scorch'd the Snake, not kill'd it:

Shee'le close, and be her selfe, whilest our poore Mallice
Remaines in danger of her former Tooth.
But let the frame of things dis-joynt,
Both the Worlds suffer,
Ere we will eate our Meale in feare, and sleepe
In the affliction of these terrible Dreames,
That shake us Nightly: Better be with the dead,
Whom we, to gayne our peace, have sent to peace,
Then on the torture of the Minde to lye
In restlesse extasie.
Duncane is in his Grave:
After Lifes fitfull Fever, he sleepes well,
Treason ha's done his worst: nor Steele, nor Poyson,
Mallice domestique, forraine Levie, nothing,
Can touch him further.
   Lady. Come on:
Gentle my Lord, sleeke o're your rugged Lookes,
Be bright and Joviall among your Guests to Night.
   Macb. So shall I Love, and so I pray be you:
Let your remembrance apply to *Banquo*,
Present him Eminence, both with Eye and Tongue:
Unsafe the while, that we must lave
Our Honors in these flattering streames,
And make our faces Vizards to our Hearts,
Disguising what they are.
   Lady. You must leave this.
   Macb. O, full of Scorpions is my Minde, deare Wife:
Thou know'st, that *Banquo* and his *Fleans* lives.
   Lady. But in them, Nature's Coppie's not eterne.
   Macb. There's comfort yet, they are assaileable,
Then be thou jocund: ere the Bat hath flowne
His Cloyster'd flight, ere to black *Heccats* summons
The shard-borne Beetle, with his drowsie hums,
Hath rung Nights yawning Peale,
There shall be done a deed of dreadfull note.
   Lady. What's to be done?
   Macb. Be innocent of the knowledge, dearest Chuck,

[66]

Till thou applaud the deed: Come, seeling Night,
Skarfe up the tender Eye of pittifull Day,
And with thy bloodie and invisible Hand
Cancell and teare to pieces that great Bond,
Which keepes me pale. Light thickens,
And the Crow makes Wing toth' Rookie Wood:
Good things of Day begin to droope, and drowse,
Whiles Nights black Agents to their Prey's doe rowse.
Thou marvell'st at my words: but hold thee still,
Things bad begun, make strong themselves by ill:
So prythee goe with me.   *Exeunt.*

Scena Tertia.

Enter three Murtherers.

   1. But who bid thee joyne with us?
   3. *Macbeth.*
   2. He needes not our mistrust, since he delivers
Our Offices, and what we have to doe,
To the direction just.
   1. Then stand with us:
The West yet glimmers with some streakes of Day.
Now spurres the lated Traveller apace,
To gayne the timely Inne, end neere approaches
The subject of our Watch.
   3. Hearke, I heare Horses.
Banquo within.   Give us a Light there, hoa.
   2. Then 'tis hee:
The rest, that are within the note of expectation,
Alreadie are i'th'Court,
   1. His Horses goe about.
   3. Almost a mile: but he does usually,
So all men doe, from hence tooth' Pallace Gate
Make it their Walke.

Enter Banquo and Fleans, with a Torch.

   2. A Light, a light.

3. 'Tis hee.

1. Stand too't.

Ban. It will be Rayne to Night

1. Let it come downe

Ban. O, Treacherie!

Flye good *Fleans*, flye, flye, flye,

Thou may'st revenge. O Slave!

3. Who did strike out the Light?

1. Was't not the way?

3. There's but one downe: the Sonne is fled.

2. We have lost

Best halfe of our Affaire.

1. Well, let's away, and say how much is done.

Exeunt.

Scena Quarta.

Banquet prepar'd. Enter Macbeth, Lady, Rosse, Lenox,
Lords, and Attendants.

Macb. You know your owne degrees, sit downe:

At first and last, the hearty welcome.

Lords. Thankes to your Majesty.

Macb. Our selfe will mingle with Society,

And play the humble Host:

Our Hostesse keepes her State, but in best time

We will require her welcome.

La. Pronounce it for me Sir, to all our Friends,

For my heart speakes, they are welcome.

Enter first Murtherer.

Macb. See they encounter thee with their harts thanks

Both Sides are even: heere Ile sit i'th'mid'st,

Be large in mirth, anon wee'l drinke a Measure

The Table round. There's blood upon thy face.

Mur. 'Tis *Banquo's* then.

Macb. 'Tis better thee without, then he within.

Is he dispatch'd?

Mur. My Lord his throat is cut, that I did for him.

Mac. Thou art the best o'th'Cut-throats,
Yet hee's good that did the like for *Fleans*:
If thou did'st it, thou art the Non-pareill.

Mur. Most Royall Sir
Fleans is scap'd.

Macb. Then comes my Fit againe:
I had else beene perfect;
Whole as the Marble, founded as the Rocke,
As broad, and generall, as the casing Ayres:
But now I am cabin d, crib'd, confin'd, bound in
To sawcy doubts, and feares. But *Banquo's* safe?

Mur. I, my good Lord: safe in a ditch he bides,
With twenty trenched gashes on his head;
The least a Death to Nature.

Macb. Thankes for that:
There the growne Serpent lyes, the worme that's fled
Hath Nature that in time will Venom breed,
No teeth for th'present. Get thee gone, to morrow
Wee'l heare our selves againe.   *Exit Murderer.*

Lady. My Royall Lord,
You do not give the Cheere, the Feast is sold
That is not often vouch'd, while 'tis a making:
'Tis given, with welcome: to feede were best at home:
From thence, the sawce to meate is Ceremony,
Meeting were bare without it.

Enter the Ghost of Banquo, and sits in Macbeths place.

Macb. Sweet Remembrancer:
Now good digestion waite on Appetite,
And health on both.

Lenox. May't please your Highnesse sit.

Macb. Here had we now our Countries Honor, roof'd,
Were the grac'd person of our *Banquo* present:
Who, may I rather challenge for unkindnesse,
Then pitty for Mischance.

Rosse. His absence (Sir)

[69]

Layes blame upon his promise. Pleas't your Highnesse
To grace us with your Royall Company?

Macb. The Table's full.

Lenox. Heere is a place reserv'd Sir.

Macb. Where?

Lenox. Heere my good Lord.
What is't that moves your Highnesse?

Macb. Which of you have done this?

Lords. What, my good Lord?

Macb. Thou canst not say I did it: never shake
Thy goary lockes at me.

Rosse. Gentlemen rise, his Highnesse is not well.

Lady. Sit worthy Friends: my Lord is often thus,
And hath beene from his youth. Pray you keepe Seat,
The fit is momentary, upon a thought
He will againe be well. If much you note him
You shall offend him, and extend his Passion,
Feed, and regard him not. Are you a man?

Macb. I, and a bold one, that dare looke on that
Which might appall the Divell.

La. O proper stuffe:
This is the very painting of your feare:
This is the Ayre-drawne-Dagger which you said
Led you to *Duncan.* O, these flawes and starts
(Imposters to true feare) would well become
A womans story, at a Winters fire
Authoriz'd by her Grandam: shame it selfe,
Why do you make such faces? When all's done
You looke but on a stoole.

Macb. Prythee see there:
Behold, looke, loe, how say you:
Why what care I, if thou canst nod, speake too.
If Charnell houses, and our Graves must send
Those that we bury, backe; our Monuments
Shall be the Mawes of Kytes.

La. What? quite unmann'd in folly.

Macb. If I stand heere, I saw him.

[70]

La. Fie for shame.

Macb. Blood hath bene shed ere now, i'th'olden time
Ere humane Statute purg'd the gentle Weale:
I, and since too, Murthers have bene perform'd
Too terrible for the eare. The times has bene,
That when the Braines were out, the man would dye,
And there an end: But now they rise againe
With twenty mortall murthers on their crownes,
And push us from our stooles. This is more strange
Then such a murther is.

La. My worthy Lord
Your Noble Friends do lacke you.

Macb. I do forget:
Do not muse at me most worthy Friends,
I have a strange infirmity, which is nothing
To those that know me. Come, love and health to all,
Then Ile sit downe: Give me some Wine, fill full:

Enter Ghost.

I drinke to th'generall joy o'th'whole Table,
And to our deere Friend *Banquo*, whom we misse:
Would he were heere: to all, and him we thirst,
And all to all.

Lords. Our duties, and the pledge.

Mac. Avant, & quit my sight, let the earth hide thee:
Thy bones are marrowlesse, thy blood is cold:
Thou hast no speculation in those eyes
Which thou dost glare with.

La. Thinke of this goode Peeres
But as a thing of Custome: 'Tis no other,
Onely it spoyles the pleasure of the time.

Macb. What man dare, I dare:
Approach thou like the rugged Russian Beare,
The arm'd Rhinoceros, or th'Hircan Tiger,
Take any shape but that, and my firme Nerves:
Shall never tremble. Or be alive againe.
And dare me to the Desart with thy Sword:

If trembling I inhabit then, protest mee
The Baby of a Girle. Hence horrible shadow,
Unreall mock'ry hence. Why so, being gone
I am a man againe: pray you sit still.

 La. You have displac'd the mirth,
Broke the good meeting, with most admir'd disorder.

 Macb. Can such things be,
And overcome us like a Summers Clowd,
Without our speciall wonder? You make me strange
Even to the disposition that I owe,
When now I thinke you can behold such sights,
And keepe the naturall Rubie of your Cheekes,
When mine is blanch'd with feare.

 Rosse. What sights my Lord?

 La. I pray you speake not: he growes worse & worse
Question enrages him: at once, goodnight.
Stand not upon the order of your going,
But go at once.

 Len. Good night, and better health
Attend his Majesty.

 La. A kinde goodnight to all.   *Exit Lords.*

 Macb. It will have blood they say:
Blood will have Blood:
Stones have beene knowne to move, & Trees to speake:
Augures, and understood Relations, have
By Maggot Pyes, & Choughes, & Rookes brought forth
The secret'st man of Blood. What is the night?

 La. Almost at oddes with morning, which is which.

 Macb. How say'st thou that *Macduff* denies his person
At our great bidding.

 La. Did you send to him Sir?

 Macb. I heare it by the way: But I will send:
There's not a one of them but in his house
I keepe a Servant Feed. I will to morrow
(And betimes I will) to the weyard Sisters.
More shall they speake: for now I am bent to know
By the worst means, the worst, for mine owne good,

All causes shall give way. I am in blood
Stept in so farre, that should I wade no more,
Returning were as tedious as go ore:
Strange things I have in head, that will to hand,
Which must be acted, ere they may be scand.

   La. You lacke the season of all Natures, sleepe.

   Macb. Come, wee'l to sleepe: my strange & self-abuse
Is the initiate feare, that wants hard use:
We are yet but yong indeed.   *Exeunt.*

Scena Quinta.

*Thunder. Enter the three Witches, meeting
Hecat.*

   1. Why how now *Hecat*, you looke angerly?

   Hec. Have I not reason (Beldams) as you are?
Sawcy, and over-bold, how did you dare
To Trade, and Trafficke with *Macbeth*,
In Riddles, and Affaires of death;
And I the Mistris of your Charmes,
The close contriver of all harmes,
Was never call'd to beare my part,
Or shew the glory of our Art?
And which is worse, all you have done
Hath bene but for a wayward Sonne,
Spightfull, and wrathfull, who (as others do)
Loves for his owne ends, not for you.
But make amends now: Get you gon,
And at the pit of Acheron
Meete me i'th'Morning: thither he
Will come, to know his Destinie.
Your Vessels, and your Spels provide,
Your Charmes, and every thing beside;
I am for th'Ayre: This night Ile spend
Unto a dismall, and a Fatall end.
Great businesse must be wrought ere Noone
Upon the Corner of the Moone

There hangs a vap'rous drop, profound,
Ile catch it ere it come to ground;
And that distill'd by Magicke slights,
Shall raise such Artificiall Sprights,
As by the strength of their illusion,
Shall draw him on to his Confusion.
He shall spurne Fate, scorne Death, and beare
His hopes 'bove Wisedome, Grace, and Feare:
And you all know, Security
Is Mortals cheefest Enemie.

Musicke, and a Song.

Hearke, I am call'd: my little Spirit see
Sits in a Foggy cloud, and stayes for me.

Sing within. Come away, come away, &c.

1 Come, lets make hast, shee'l soone be
Backe againe.   *Exeunt.*

Scena Sexta.

Enter Lenox, and another Lord.

Lenox. My former Speeches,
Have but hit your Thoughts
Which can interpret farther: Onely I say
Things have bin strangely borne. The gracious *Duncan*
Was pittied of *Macbeth*: marry he was dead:
And the right valiant *Banquo* walk'd too late,
Whom you may say (if't please you) *Fleans* kill'd,
For *Fleans* fled: Men must not walke too late.
Who cannot want the thought, how monstrous
It was for *Malcolme*, and for *Donalbane*
To kill their gracious Father? Damned Fact,
How it did greeve *Macbeth*? Did he not straight
In pious rage, the two delinquents teare,
That were the Slaves of drinke, and thralles of sleepe?
Was not that Nobly done? I, and wisely too:
For 'twould have anger'd any heart alive
To heare the men deny't. So that I say,

[74]

He ha's borne all things well, and I do thinke,
That had he *Duncans* Sonnes under his Key,
(As, and't please Heaven he shall not) they should finde
What 'twere to kill a Father: So should *Fleans*.
But peace; for from broad words, and cause he fayl'd
His presence at the Tyrants Feast, I heare
Macduffe lives in disgrace. Sir, can you tell
Where he bestowes himselfe?

    Lord. The Sonnes of *Duncane*
(From whom this Tyrant holds the due of Birth)
Lives in the English Court, and is receyv'd
Of the most Pious *Edward*, with such grace,
That the malevolence of Fortune, nothing
Takes from his high respect. Thither *Macduffe*
Is gone, to pray the Holy King, upon his ayd
To wake Northumberland, and warlike *Seyward*,
That by the helpe of these (with him above)
To ratifie the Worke) we may againe
Give to our Tables meate, sleepe to our Nights:
Free from our Feasts, and Banquets bloody knives;
Do faithfull Homage, and receive free Honors,
All which we pine for now. And this report
Hath so exasperate their King, that hee
Prepares for some attempt of Warre.

    Len. Sent he to *Macduffe*?

    Lord. He did: and with an absolute Sir, not I
The clowdy Messenger turnes me his backe,
And hums; as who should say, you'l rue the time
That clogges me with this Answer.

    Lenox. And that well might
Advise him to a Caution, t hold what distance
His wisedome can provide. Some holy Angell
Flye to the Court of England, and unfold
His message ere he come, that a swift blessing
May soone returne to this our suffering Country,
Under a hand accurs'd.

    Lord. Ile send my Prayers with him.   *Exeunt*

The Tragedie of Macbeth
Actus Quartus. Scena Prima.

Thunder. Enter the three Witches.

1 Thrice the brinded Cat hath mew'd.

2 Thrice, and once the Hedge-Pigge whin'd.

3 Harpier cries, 'tis time, 'tis time.

1 Round about the Caldron go:
In the poysond Entrailes throw
Toad, that under cold stone,
Dayes and Nights, ha's thirty one:
Sweltred Venom sleeping got,
Boyle thou first i'th'charmed pot.

All. Double, double, toile and trouble;
Fire burne, and Cauldron bubble.

2 Fillet of a Fenny Snake,
In the Cauldron boyle and bake:
Eye of Newt, and Toe of Frogge,
Wooll of Bat, and Tongue of Dogge:
Adders Forke, and Blinde-wormes Sting,
Lizards legge, and Howlets wing:
Like a Hell-broth, boyle and bubble.

All. Double, double, toyle and trouble,
Fire burne, and Cauldron bubble.

3 Scale of Dragon, Tooth of Wolfe,
Witches Mummey, Maw, and Gulfe
Of the ravin'd salt Sea sharke:
Roote of Hemlocke, digg'd i'th'darke:
Liver of Blaspheming Jew,
Gall of Goate, and Slippes of Yew,
Sliver'd in the Moones Ecclipse:
Nose of Turke, and Tartars lips:
Finger of Birth-strangled Babe,
Ditch-deliver'd by a Drab,
Make the Grewell thicke, and slab
Adde thereto a Tigers Chawdron,
For th'Ingredience of our Cawdron.

All. Double, double, toyle and trouble,

Fire burne, and Cauldron bubble.

  2 Coole it with a Baboones blood,
Then the Charme is firme and good.

Enter Hecat, and the other three Witches.

  Hec. O well done: I commend your paines,
And every one shall share i'th'gaines:
And now about the Cauldron sing
Like Elves and Fairies in a Ring,
Inchanting all that you put in.
Musicke and a Song. Blacke Spirits, &c.

  2 By the pricking of my Thumbes,
Something wicked this way comes:
Open Lockes, who ever knockes.

Enter Macbeth.

  Macb. How now you secret, black, & midnight Hags?
What is't you do?
  All. A deed without a name.
  Macb. I conjure you, by that which you Professe,
(How ere you come to know it) answer me:
Though you untye the Windes, and let them fight
Against the Churches: Though the yesty Waves
Confound and swallow Navigation up:
Though bladed Corne be lodg'd, & Trees blown downe,
Though Castles topple on their Warders heads:
Though Pallaces, and Pyramids do slope
Their heads to their Foundations: Though the treasure
Of Natures Germaine, tumble altogether,
Even till destruction sicken: Answer me
To what I aske you.
  1 Speake.
  2 Demand.
  3 Wee'l answer.
  1 Say, if th'hadst rather heare it from our mouthes,
Or from our Masters.
  Macb. Call 'em: let me see 'em.

1 Powre in Sowes blood, that hath eaten
Her nine Farrow: Greaze that's sweaten
From the Murderers Gibbet, throw
Into the Flame.

All. Come high or low:
Thy selfe and Office deaftly show.   *Thunder.*

                    1. Apparation, an Armed Head.

Macb. Tell me, thou unknowne power.

1 He knowes thy thought:
Heare his speech, but say thou nought.

1 *Appar. Macbeth, Macbeth, Macbeth:*
Beware *Macduffe*,
Beware the Thane of Fife: dismisse me. Enough.

                              He Descends.

Macb. What ere thou art, for thy good caution, thanks
Thou hast harp'd my feare aright. But one word more.

1 He will not be commanded: heere's another
More potent then the first.   *Thunder.*

                    2 Apparition, a Bloody Childe.

2 *Appar. Macbeth, Macbeth, Macbeth.*

Macb. Had I three eares, Il'd heare thee.

2 *Appar Appar.* Be bloody, bold, & resolute:
Laugh to scorne
The powre of man: For none of woman borne
Shall harme *Macbeth.*   *Descends.*

Mac. Then live *Macduffe*: what need I feare of thee?
But yet Ile make assurance: double sure,
And take a Bond of Fate: thou shalt not live,
That I may tell pale-hearted Feare, it lies;
And sleepe in spight of Thunder.   *Thunder.*

3 *Apparition, a Childe Crowned, with a Tree in his hand.*
What is this, that rises like the issue of a King,
And weares upon his Baby-brow, the round
And top of Soveraignty?

All. Listen, but speake not too't.

3 *Appar.* Be Lyon metled, proud, and take no care:
Who chases, who frets, or where Conspirers are:

Macbeth shall never vanquish'd be, untill
Great Byrnam Wood, to high *Dunsmane* Hill
Shall come against him.   *Descends.*

  Macb. That will never bee:
Who can impresse the Forrest, bid the Tree
Unfixe his earth-bound Root? Sweet boadments, good:
Rebellious dead, rise never till the Wood
Of Byrnan rise, and our high plac'd *Macbeth*
Shall live the Lease of Nature, pay his breath
To time, and mortall Custome. Yet my Hart
Throbs to know one thing: Tell me, if your Art
Can tell so much: Shall *Banquo's* issue ever
Reigne in this Kingdome?
  All. Seeke to know no more.
  Macb. I will be satisfied. Deny me this,
And an eternall Curse fall on you: Let me know!
Why sinkes that Caldron? & what noise is this? *Hoboyes.*
  1 Shew.
  2 Shew.
  3 Shew.
  All. Shew his Eyes, and greeve his Hart,
Come like shadowes, so depart.

    *A shew of Eight Kings, and Banquo last, with a glasse
              in his hand.*

  Macb. Thou art too like the Spirit of *Banquo*: Down:
Thy Crowne do's seare mine Eye-bals. And thy haire
Thou other Gold-bound-brow, is like the first:
A third, is like the former. Filthy Hagges,
Why do you shew me this? ------ A fourth? Start eyes!
What will the Line stretch out to'th'cracke of Doome?
Another yet? A seaventh? Ile see no more:
And yet the eight appeares, who beares a glasse,
Which shewes me many more: and some I see,
That two-fold Balles, and trebble Scepters carry.
Horrible sight: now I see 'tis true,
For the Blood-bolter'd *Banquo* smiles upon me,

And points at them for his. What? is this so?

   1 I Sir, all this is so. But why
Stands *Macbeth* Thus amazedly?
Come Sisters, cheere we up his sprights,
And shew the best of our delights.
Ile Charme the Ayre to give a sound,
While you performe your Antique round:
That this great King may kindly say,
Our duties, did his welcome pay.   *Musicke.*

The Witches Dance, and Vanish.

  Macb. Where are they? Gone?
Let this pernitious houre,
Stand aye accursed in the Kalender.
Come in, without there.   *Enter Lenox.*

  Lenox. What's your Graces will.

  Macb. Saw you the Weyward Sisters?

  Lenox. No my Lord.

  Macb. Came they not by you?

  Lenox. No indeed my Lord.

  Macb. Infected be the Ayre whereon they ride,
And damn'd all those that trust them. I did heare
The gallopping of Horse. Who was't came by?

  Len. 'Tis two or three my Lord, that bring you word:
Macduff is fled to England.

  Macb. Fled to England?

  Len. I, my good Lord.

  Macb. Time, thou anticipat'st my dread exploits:
The flighty purpose never is o're-tooke
Unlesse the deed go with it. From this moment,
The very firstlings of my heart shall be
The firstlings of my hand. And even now
To Crown my thoughts with Acts: be it thoght & done:
The Castle of *Macduff*, I will surprize,
Seize upon Fife: give to th'edge o'th'Sword
His Wife, his Babes, and all unfortunate Soules
That trace him in his Line. No boasting like a Foole,

This deed Ile do, before this purpose coole,
But no more sights. Where are these Gentlemen?
Come bring me where they are. *Exeunt.*

Scena Secunda.

Enter Macduffes Wife, her Son, and Rosse.

Wife. What had he done, to make him fly the Land?
Rosse. You must have patience Madam.
Wife. He had none:
His flight was madnesse: when our Actions do not,
Our feares do make us Traitors.
Rosse. You know not
Whether it was his wisedome, or his feare.
Wife. Wisedome? to leave his wife, to leave his Babes,
His Mansion, and his Titles, in a place
From whence himselfe do's flye? He loves us not,
He wants the naturall touch. For the poore Wren
(The most diminitive of Birds) will fight,
Her yong ones in her Nest, against the Owle:
All is the Feare, and nothing is the Love;
As little is the Wisedome, where the flight
So runnes against all reason.
Rosse. My deerest Cooz,
I pray you schoole your selfe. But for your Husband,
He is Noble, Wise, Judicious, and best knowes
The fits o'th'Season. I dare not speake much further,
But cruell are the times, when we are Traitors
And do not know our selves: when we hold Rumor
From what we feare, yet know not what we feare,
But floate upon a wilde and violent Sea
Each way, and move. I take my leave of you:
Shall not be long but Ile be heere againe:
Things at the worst will cease, or else climbe upward,
To what they were before. My pretty Cosine,
Blessing upon you.
Wife. Father'd he is,

And yet hee's Father-lesse.

Rosse. I am so much a Foole, should I stay longer
It would be my disgrace, and your discomfort.
I take my leave at once.   *Exit Rosse.*

Wife. Sirra, your Fathers dead,
And what will you do now? How will you live?

Son. As Birds do Mother.

Wife. What with Wormes, and Flyes?

Son. With what I get I meane, and so do they.

Wife. Poore Bird,
Thou'dst never Feare the Net, nor Lime,
The Pitfall, nor the Gin.

Son. Why should I Mother?
Poore Birds they are not set for:
My Father is not dead for all your saying.

Wife. Yes, he is dead:
How wilt thou do for a Father?

Son. Nay how will you do for a Husband?

Wife. Why I can buy me twenty at any Market.

Son. Then you'l by 'em to sell againe.

Wife. Thou speak'st withall thy wit,
And yet I'faith with wit enough for thee.

Son. Was my Father a Traitor, Mother?

Wife. I, that he was.

Son. What is this a Traitor?

Wife. Why one that sweares, and lyes.

Son. And be all Traitors, that do so.

Wife. Every one that do's so, is a Traitor,
And must be hang'd.

Son. And must they all be hang'd, that sweare and lye?

Wife. Every one.

Son. Who must hang them?

Wife. Why, the honest men.

Son. Then the Liars and Swearers are Fools: for there are
Lyars and Swearers enow, to beate the honest men, and hang
up them.

Wife. Now God helpe thee, poore Monkie:

[82]

But how wilt thou do for a Father?

Son. If he were dead, youl'd weepe for him: if you would
not, it were a good signe, that I should quickely have a new
Father.

Wife. Poore pratler, how thou talk'st?

Enter a Messenger.

Mes. Blesse you faire Dame: I am not to you known,
Though in your state of Honor I am perfect;
I doubt some danger do's approach you neerely.
If you will take a homely mans advice,
Be not found heere: Hence with your little ones
To fright you thus. Me thinkes I am too savage:
To do worse to you were fell Cruelty,
Which is too nie your person. Heaven preserve you,
I dare abide no longer.   *Exit Messenger*

Wife. Whether should I flye?
I have done no harme. But I remember now
I am in this earthly world: where to do harme
Is often laudable, to do good sometime
Accounted dangerous folly. Why then (alas)
Do I put up that womanly defence,
To say I have done no harme?
What are these faces?

Enter Murtherers.

Mur. Where is your Husband?

Wife. I hope in no place so unsanctified,
Where such as thou may'st finde him.

Mur. He's a Traitor.

Son. Thou ly'st thou shagge-ear'd Villaine.

Mur. What you Egge?
Yong fry of Treachery?

Son. He ha's kill'd me Mother,
Run away I pray you.   *Exit crying Murther.*

Scena Tertia.

Enter Malcolme and Macduffe.

Mal. Let us seeke out some desolate shade, & there
Weepe our sad bosomes empty.

Macd. Let us rather
Hold fast the mortall Sword: and like good men,
Bestride our downfall Birthdome: each new Morne,
New Widdowes howle, new Orphans cry, new sorowes
Strike heaven on the face, that it resounds
As if it felt with Scotland, and yell'd out
Like Syllable of Dolour.

Mal. What I beleeve, Ile waile;
What know, beleeve; and what I can redresse,
As I shall finde the time to friend: I wil.
What you have spoke, it may be so perchance.
This Tyrant, whose sole name blisters our tongues,
Was once thought honest: you have lov'd him well,
He hath not touch'd you yet. I am yong, but something
You may discerne of him through me, and wisedome
To offer up a weake, poore innocent Lambe
T'appease an angry God.

Macd. I am not treacherous.

Malc. But *Macbeth* is.
A good and vertuous Nature may recoyle
In an Imperiall charge. But I shall crave your pardon:
That which you are, my thoughts cannot transpose;
Angels are bright still, though the brightest fell.
Though all things foule, would wear the brows of grace
Yet Grace must still looke so.

Macd. I have lost my Hopes.

Malc. Perchance even there
Where I did finde my doubts.
Why in that rawnesse left you Wife, and Child?
Those precious Motives, those strong knots of Love,
Without leave-taking. I pray you,
Let not my Jealousies, be your Dishonors,
But mine owne Safeties: you may be rightly just,
What ever I shall thinke.

Macd. Bleed, bleed poore Country,

Great Tyrrany, lay thou thy basis sure,
For goodnesse dare not check thee: wear ye thy wrongs,
The Title, is affear'd. Far thee well Lord,
I would not be the Villaine that thou think'st,
For the whole Space that's in the Tyrants Graspe,
And the rich East to boot.

Mal. Be not offended:
I speake not as in absolute feare of you:
I thinke our Country sinkes beneath the yoake,
It weepes, it bleeds, and each new day a gash
Is added to her wounds. I thinke withall,
There would be hands uplifted in my right:
And heere from gracious England have I offer
Of goodly thousands. But for all this,
When I shall treade upon the Tyrants head,
Or weare it on my Sword; yet my poore Country
Shall have more vices then it had before,
More suffer, and more sundry wayes then ever,
By him that shall succeede.

Macd. What should he be?

Mal. It is my selfe I meane: in whom I knowe
All the particulars of Vice so grafted,
That when they shall be open'd, blacke *Macbeth*
Will seeme as pure as Snow, and the poore State
Esteeme him as a Lambe, being compar'd
With my confinelesse harmes.

Macd. Not in the Legions
Of horrid Hell, can come a Divell more damn'd
In evils, to top *Macbeth*.

Mal. I grant him Bloody,
Luxurious, Avaricious, False, Deceitfull,
Sodaine, Malicious, smacking of every sinne
That ha's a name. But there's no bottome, none
In my Voluptuousnesse: Your wives, your Daughters,
Your Matrons, and your Maides, could not fill up
The Cesterne of my Lust, and my Desire
All continent Impediments would ore-beare

[85]

That did oppose my will. Better *Macbeth*,
Then such an one to reigne.
   Macd. Boundlesse intemperance
In Nature is a Tyranny: It hath beene
Th'untimely emptying of the happy Throne,
And fall of many Kings. But feare not yet
To take upon you what is yours: you may
Convey your pleasures in a spacious plenty,
And yet seeme cold. The time you may so hoodwinke:
We have willing Dames enough: there cannot be
That Vulture in you, to devoure so many
As will to Greatnesse dedicate themselves,
Finding it so inclinde.
   Mal. With this, there growes
In my most ill-compos d Affection, such
A stanchlesse Avarice, that were I King
I should cut off the Nobles for their Lands,
Desire his Jewels, and this others House,
And my more-having, would be as a Sawce
To make me hunger more, that I should forge
Quarrels unjust against the Good and Loyall,
Destroying them for wealth,
   Macd. This Avarice
stickes deeper: growes with more pernicious roote
Then Summer-seeming Lust: and it hath bin
The Sword of our slaine Kings: yet do not feare,
Scotland hath Foysons, to fill up your will
Of your meere Owne. All these are portable,
With other Graces weigh'd.
   Mal. But I have none. The King becoming Graces,
As Justice, Verity, Temp'rance, Stablenesse,
Bounty. Perseverance, Mercy, Lowlinesse,
Devotion, Patience, Courage, Fortitude,
I have no rellish of them, but abound
In the division of each severall Crime,
Acting it many wayes. Nay, had I powre, I should
Poure the sweet Milke of Concord, into Hell,

Uprore the universall peace, confound
All unity on earth.

   Macd. O Scotland, Scotland.

   Mal. If such a one be fit to governe, speake:
I am as I have spoken.

   Mac. Fit to govern? No not to live. O Nation miserable!
With an untitled Tyrant, bloody Sceptred,
When shalt thou see thy wholsome dayes againe?
Since that the truest Issue of thy Throne
By his owne Interdiction stands accust,
And do's blaspheme his breed? Thy Royall Father
Was a most Sainted-King: the Queene that bore thee,
Oftner upon her knees, then on her feet,
Dy'de every day she liv'd. Fare thee well,
These Evils thou repeat'st upon thy selfe,
Hath banish'd me from Scotland. O my Brest,
Thy hope ends heere.

   Mal. Macduff, this Noble passion
Childe of integrity, hath from my soule
Wip'd the blacke Scruples, reconcil'd my thoughts
To thy good Truth, and Honor. Divellish *Macbeth,*
By many of these traines, hath sought to win me
Into his power: and modest Wisedome pluckes me
From over-credulous hast: but God above
Deale betweene thee and me; For even now
I put my selfe to thy Direction, and
Unspeake mine owne detraction. Heere abjure
The taints, and blames I laide upon my selfe,
For strangers to my Nature. I am yet
Unknowne to Woman, never was forsworne,
Scarsely have coveted what was mine owne:
At no time broke my Faith, would not betray
The Devill to his Fellow, and delight
No lesse in truth then life. My first false speaking
Was this upon my selfe. What I am truly
Is thine, and my poore Countries to command:
Whither indeed, before they heere approach

Old *Seyward* with ten thousand warlike men
Already at a point, was setting foorth:
Now wee'l togther, and the chance of goodnesse
Be like our warranted Quarrell. Why are you silent?
  Macd. Such welcome, and unwelcome things at once
'Tis hard to reconcile.

Enter a Doctor.

  Mal. Well, more anon. Comes the King forth
I pray you?
  Doct. I Sir: there are a crew of wretched Soules
That stay his Cure: their malady convinces
The great assay of Art. But at his touch,
Such sanctity hath Heaven given his hand,
They presently amend.   *Exit.*
  Mal. I thanke you Doctor.
  Macd. What's the Disease he meanes?
  Mal. Tis call'd the Evill.
A most myraculous worke in this good King,
Which often since my heere remaine in England,
I have seene him do: How he solicites heaven
Himselfe best knowes: but strangely visited people
All swolne and Ulcerous, pittifull to the eye,
The meere dispaire of Surgery, he cures,
Hanging a golden stampe about their neckes,
Put on with holy Prayers, and 'tis spoken
To the succeeding Royalty he leaves
The healing Benediction. With this strange vertue,
He hath a heavenly guift of Prophesie,
And sundry Blessings hang about his Throne,
That speake him full of Grace.

Enter Rosse.

  Macd. See who comes heere.
  Malc. My Countryman: but yet I know him not.
  Macd. My ever gentle Cozen, welcome hither.

Malc. I know him now. Good God betimes remove
The meanes that makes us Strangers.

Rosse. Sir, Amen.

Macd. Stands Scotland where it did?

Rosse. Alas poore Countrey,
Almost affraid to know it selfe. It cannot
Be call'd our Mother, but our Grave; where nothing
But who knowes nothing, is once seene to smile:
Where sighes, and groanes, and shrieks that rent the ayre
Are made, not mark'd: Where violent sorrow seemes
A Moderne extasie: The Deadmans knell,
Is there scarse ask'd for who, and good mens lives
Expire before the Flowers in their Caps,
Dying, or ere they sicken.

Macd. Oh Relation; to nice, and yet too true.

Malc. What's the newest griefe?

Rosse. That of an houres age, doth hisse the speaker,
Each minute teemes a new one.

Macd. How do's my Wife?

Rosse. Why well.

Macd. And all my Children?

Rosse. Well too.

Macd. The Tyrant ha's not batter'd at their peace?

Rosse. No, they were wel at peace, when I did leave 'em.

Macd. Be not a niggard of your speech: How gos't?

Rosse. When I came hither to transport the Tydings
Which I have heavily borne, there ran a Rumour
Of many worthy Fellowes, that were out,
Which was to my beleefe witnest the rather,
For that I saw the Tyrants Power a-foot.
Now is the time of helpe: your eye in Scotland
Would create Soldiours, make our women fight,
To doffe their dire distresses.

Malc. Bee't their comfort
We are comming thither: Gracious England hath
Lent us good *Seyward*, and ten thousand men,
An older, and a better Souldier, none

That Christendome gives out.

   Rosse. Would I could answer
This comfort with the like. But I have words
That would be howl'd out in the desert ayre,
Where hearing should not latch them.

   Macd. What concerne they,
The generall cause, or is it a Fee-griefe
Due to some single brest?

   Rosse. No minde that's honest
But in it shares some woe, though the maine part
Pertaines to you alone.

   Macd. If it be mine
Keepe it not from me, quickly let me have it.

   Rosse. Let not your eares dispise my tongue for ever,
Which shall possesse them with the heaviest sound
That ever yet they heard.

   Macd. Humh: I guesse at it.

   Rosse. Your Castle is surpriz'd: your Wife, and Babes
Savagely slaughter'd: To relate the manner
Were on the Quarry of these murther'd Deere
To adde the death of you.

   Malc. Mercifull Heaven:
What man, ne're pull your hat upon your browes:
Give sorrow words; the griefe that do's not speake,
Whispers the o're-fraught heart, and bids it breake.

   Macd. My Children too?

   Ro. Wife, Children, Servants, all that could be found.

   Macd. And I must be from thence? My wife kil'd too?

   Rosse. I have said.

   Malc. Be comforted.
Let's make us Med'cines of our great Revenge,
To cure this deadly greefe.

   Macd. He ha's no Children. All my pretty ones?
Did you say All? Oh Hell-Kite! All?
What, All my pretty Chickens, and their Damme
At one fell swoope?

   Malc. Dispute it like a man.

Macd. I shall do so:
But I must also feele it as a man;
I cannot but remember such things were
That were most precious to me: Did heaven looke on,
And would not take their part? Sinfull *Macduff*,
They were all strooke for thee: Naught that I am,
Not for their owne demerits, but for mine
Fell slaughter on their soules: Heaven rest them now.

Mal. Be this the Whetstone of your sword, let griefe
Convert to anger: blunt not the heart, enrage it.

Macd. O I could play the woman with mine eyes,
And Braggart with my tongue. But gentle Heavens,
Cut short all intermission: Front to Front,
Bring thou this Fiend of Scotland, and my selfe
Within my Swords length set him, if he scape
Heaven forgive him too.

Mal. This time goes manly:
Come go we to the King, our Power is ready,
Our lacke is nothing but our leave. *Macbeth*
Is ripe for shaking, and the Powres above
Put on their Instruments: Receive what cheere you may,
The Night is long, that never findes the Day.   *Exeunt.*

Actus Quintus. Scena Prima.

*Enter a Doctor of Physicke, and a Wayting
Gentlewoman.*

Doct. I have too Nights watch'd with you, but can perceive no truth in your report. When was it shee last walk'd.

Gent. Since his Majesty went into the Field, I have seene her rise from her bed, throw her Night-Gown uppon her, unlocke her Closset, take foorth paper, folde it, write upon't, read it, afterwards Seale it, and againe returne to bed; yet all this while in a most fast sleepe.

Doct. A great perturbation in Nature, to receyve at once the benefit of sleep, and do the effects of watching. In this slumbry agitation, besides her walking, and other actuall performances, what (at any time) have you heard her say?

Gent. That Sir, which I will not report after her.

Doct. You may to me, and 'tis most meet you should.

Gent. Neither to you, nor any one, having no witnesse to confirme my speech.   *Enter Lady, with a Taper.*

Lo you, heere she comes: This is her very guise, and upon my life fast asleepe: observe her, stand close.

Doct. How came she by that light?

Gent. Why it stood by her: she ha's light by her continually, 'tis her command.

Doct. You see her eyes are open.

Gent. I but their sense are shut.

Doct. What is it she do's now? Looke how she rubbes her hands.

Gent. It is an accustom'd action with her, to seeme thus washing her hands: I have knowne her to continue in this a quarter of an houre.

Lad. Yet heere's a spot.

Doct. Heark, she speakes, I will set downe what comes from her, to satisfie my remembrance the more strongly.

La. Out damned spot: out I say. One: Two: Why then 'tis time to doo't: Hell is murky. Fye, my Lord, fie, a Souldier, and affear'd? what need we feare? who knowes it, when none can call our powre to accompt: yet who would have thought the olde man to have so much blood in him.

Doct. Do you marke that?

Lad. The Thane of Fife, had a wife: where is she now? What will these hands ne're be cleane? No more o'that my Lord, no more o'that: you marre all with this starting.

Doct. Go too, go too: You have knowne what you should not.

Gent. She ha's spoke what shee should not, I am sure of that: Heaven knowes what she ha's knowne.

[92]

La. Heere's the smell of the blood still: all the perfumes of Arabia will not sweeten this little hand. Oh. oh, oh.

Doct. What a sigh is there? The hart is sorely charg'd.

Gent. I would not have such a heart in my bosome, for the dignity of the whole body.

Doct. Well, well, well.

Gent. Pray God it be sir.

Doct. This disease is beyond my practise: yet I have knowne those which have walkt in their sleep, who have dyed holily in their beds.

Lad. Wash your hands, put on your Night-Gowne, looke not so pale: I tell you yet againe *Banquo's* buried; he cannot come out on's grave.

Doct. Even so?

Lady. To bed, to bed: there's knocking at the gate: Come, come, come, come, give me your hand: What's done, cannot be undone. To bed, to bed, to bed.

Exit Lady.

Doct. Will she go now to bed?

Gent. Directly.

Doct. Foule whisp'rings are abroad: unnaturall deeds
Do breed unnaturall troubles: infected mindes
To their deafe pillowes will discharge their Secrets:
More needs she the Divine, then the Physitian:
God, God forgive us all. Looke after her,
Remove from her the meanes of all annoyance,
And still keepe eyes upon her: So goodnight,
My minde she ha's mated, and amaz'd my sight.
I thinke, but dare not speake.

Gent. Good night good Doctor. *Exeunt.*

Scena Secunda.

Drum and Colours. Enter Menteth, Cathnes,
Angus, Lenox, Soldiers.

Ment. The English powre is neere, led on by *Malcolm*,

His Unkle *Seyward*, and the good *Macduff.*
Revenges burne in them: for their deere causes
Would to the bleeding, and the grim Alarme
Excite the mortified man.

   Ang. Neere Byrnan wood
Shall we well meet them, that way are they comming.

   Cath. Who knowes if *Donalbane* be with his brother?

   Len. For certaine Sir, he is not: I have a File
Of all the Gentry; there is *Seywards* Sonne,
And many unruffe youths, that even now
Protest their first of Manhood.

   Ment. What do's the Tyrant.

   Cath. Great Dunsinane he strongly Fortifies
Some say hee's mad: Others, that lesser hate him,
Do call it valiant Fury, but for certaine
He cannot buckle his distemper'd cause
Within the belt of Rule.

   Ang. Now do's he feele
His secret Murthers sticking on his hands,
Now minutely Revolts upbraid his Faith-breach:
Those he commands, move onely in command,
Nothing in love: Now do's he feele his Title
Hang loose about him, like a Giants Robe
Upon a dwarfish Theefe.

   Ment. Who then shall blame
His pester'd Senses to recoyle, and start,
When all that is within him, do's condemne
It selfe, for being there.

   Cath. Well, march we on,
To give Obedience, where 'tis truly ow'd:
Meet we the Med'cine of the sickly Weale,
And with him poure we in our Countries purge,
Each drop of us.

   Lenox. Or so much as it needes,
To dew the Soveraigne Flower, and drowne the Weeds:
Make we our March towards Birnan.   *Exeunt marching.*

The Tragedie of Macbeth

Scena Tertia.

Enter Macbeth, Doctor, and Attendants.

Macb. Bring me no more Reports, let them flye all:
Till Byrnane wood remove to Dunsinane,
I cannot taint with Feare. What's the Boy *Malcolme*?
Was he not borne of woman? The Spirits that know
All mortall Consequences, have pronounc'd me thus:
Feare not *Macbeth*, no man that's borne of woman
Shall ere have power upon thee. Then fly false *Thanes*,
And mingle with the English Epicures,
The minde I sway by, and the heart I beare,
Shall never sagge with doubt, nor shake wih feare.

Enter Servant.

The divell damne thee blacke, thou cream-fac'd Loone:
Where got'st thou that Goose-looke.
    Ser. There is ten thousand.
    Macb. Geese Villaine?
    Ser. Souldiers Sir.
    Macb. Go pricke thy face, and over-red thy feare
Thou Lilly-liver'd Boy. What Soldiers, Patch?
Death of thy Soule, those Linnen cheekes of thine
Are Counsailers to feare. What Soldiers Whay-face?
    Ser. The English Force, so please you.
    Macb. Take thy face hence. *Seyton*, I am sick at hart,
When I behold: *Seyton*, I say, this push
Will cheere me ever, or dis-eate me now.
I have liv'd long enough, my way of life
Is falne into the Seare, the yellow Leafe,
And that which should accompany Old-Age,
As Honor, Love, Obedience, Troopes of Friends,
I must not looke to have: but in their steed,
Curses, not lowd but deepe, Mouth-honor, breath
Which the poore heart would faine deny, and dare not.
Seyton?

Enter Seyton.

[95]

Sey. What's your gracious pleasure?

Macb. What Newes more?

Sey. All is confirm'd my Lord, which was reported.

Macb. Ile fight, till from my bones, my flesh be hackt.
Give me my Armor.

Seyt. 'Tis not needed yet.

Macb. Ile put it on:
Send out moe Horses, skirre the Country round,
Hang those that talke of Feare. Give me mine Armor:
How do's your Patient, Doctor?

Doct. Not so sicke my Lord,
As she is troubled with thicke-comming Fancies
That keepe her from her rest.

Macb. Cure of that:
Can'st thou not Minister to a minde diseas'd,
Plucke from the Memory a rooted Sorrow,
Raze out the written troubles of the Braine,
And with some sweet Oblivious Antidote
Cleanse the stufft bosome, of that perillous stuffe
Which weighes upon the heart?

Doct. Therein the Patient
Must minister to himselfe.

Macb. Throw Physicke to the Dogs, Ile none of it.
Come, put mine Armour on: give me my Staffe:
Seyton, send out: Doctor, the Thanes flye from me:
Come sir, dispatch. If thou could'st Doctor, cast
The Water of my Land, finde her Disease,
And purge it to a sound and pristive Health,
I would applaud thee to the very Eccho,
That should applaud againe. Pull't off I say,
What Rhubarb, Cyme, or what Purgative drugge
Would scowre these English hence: hear'st y of them?

Doct. I my good Lord: your Royall Preparation
Makes us heare something.

Macb. Bring it after me:
I will not be affraid of Death and Bane,

Till Birnane Forrest come to Dunsinane.

Doct. Were I from Dunsinane away, and cleere,
Profit againe should hardly draw me heere.   *Exeunt.*

Scena Quarta.

*Drum and Colours. Enter Malcolme, Seyward, Macduffe,
Seywards Sonne, Menteth, Cathnes, Angus,
and Soldiers Marching.*

Malc. Cosins, I hope the dayes are neere at hand
That Chambers will be safe.

Ment. We doubt it nothing.

Syew. What wood is this before us?

Ment. The wood of Birnane.

Malc. Let every Souldier hew him downe a Bough,
And bear't before him, thereby shall we shadow
The numbers of our Hoast, and make discovery
Erre in report of us.

Sold. It shall be done.

Syw. We learne no other, but the confident Tyrant
Keepes still in Dunsinane, and will indure
Our setting downe befor't.

Malc. 'Tis his maine hope:
For where there is advantage to be given him the Revolt,
And none serve with him, but constrained things,
Whose hearts are absent too.

Macd. Let our just Censures
Attend the true event, and put we on
Industrious Souldiership.

Sey. The time approaches,
That will with due decision make us know
What we shall say we have, and what we owe:
Thoughts speculative, their unsure hopes relate,
But certaine issue, stroakes must arbitrate,
Towards which, advance the warre.   *Exeunt marching.*

The Tragedie of Macbeth
Scena Quinta.

Enter Macbeth, Seyton, & Souldiers, with,
Drum and Colours.

Macb. Hang out our Banners on the outward walls,
The Cry is still, they come: our Castles strength
Will laugh a Siedge to scorne: Heere let them lye,
Till Famine and the Ague eate them up:
Were they not forc'd with those that should be ours,
We might have met them darefull, beard to beard,
And beate them backward home. What is that noyse?

A Cry within of Women.

Sey. It is the cry of women, my good Lord.
Macb. I have almost forgot the taste of Feares:
The time ha's beene, my sences would have cool'd
To heare a Night-shricke, and my Fell of haire
Would at a dismall Treatise rowze, and stirre
As life were in't. I have supt full with horrors,
Direnesse familiar to my slaughterous thoughts
Cannot once start me. Wherefore was that cry?
Sey. The Queene (my Lord) is dead.
Macb. She should have dy'de heereafter;
There would have beene a time for such a word:
To morrow, and to morrow, and to morrow,
Creepes in this petty pace from day to day,
To the last Syllable of Recorded time:
And all our yesterdayes, have lighted Fooles
The way to dusty death. Out, out, breefe Candle,
Life's but a walking Shadow, a poore Player,
That struts and frets his houre upon the Stage,
And then is heard no more. It is a Tale
Told by an Ideot, full of sound and fury
Signify nothing.   *Enter a Messenger.*
Thou com'st to use thy Tongue: thy Story quickly.
Mes. Gracious Lord,
I should report that which I say I saw,
But know not how to doo't.

Macb. Well, say sir.

Mes. As I did stand my watch upon the Hill
I look'd toward Byrnane, and anon me thought
The Wood began to move.

Macb. Lyar, and Slave.

Mes. Let me endure your wrath, if't be not so:
Within this three Mile may you see it comming.
I say, a moving Grove.

Macb. If thou speak'st false,
Upon the next Tree shall thou hang alive
Till Famine cling thee: if thy speech be sooth,
I care not if thou dost for me as much.
I pull in Resolution, and begin
To doubt th'Equivocation of the Fiend,
That lies like truth. Feare not, till Byrnane Wood
Do come to Dunsinane, and now a Wood
Comes toward Dunsinane. Arme, Arme, and out,
If this which he avouches, do's appeare,
There is nor flying hence, nor tarrying here.
I'ginne to be a-weary of the Sun,
And wish th'estate o'th'world were now undon.
Ring the Alarum Bell, blow Winde, come wracke,
At least wee'l dye with Harnesse on our backe.   *Exeunt.*

Scena Sexta.

Drumme and Colours.
Enter Malcolme, Seyward, Macduffe, and their Army,
with Boughes.

Mal. Now neere enough:
Your leavy Skreenes throw downe,
And shew like those you are: You (worthy Unkle)
Shall with my Cosin your right Noble Sonne
Leade our first Battell. Worthy *Macduffe*, and wee
Shall take upon's what else remaines to do,
According to our order.

Sey. Fare you well:
Do we but finde the Tyrants power to night,
Let us be beaten, if we cannot fight.
  Macd. Make all our Trumpets speak, give them all breath
Those clamorous Harbingers of Blood, & Death.   *Exeunt.*
                                        Alarums continued.

Scena Septima.

Enter Macbeth.

  Macb. They have tied me to a stake, I cannot flye,
But Beare-like I must fight the course. What's he
That was not borne of Woman? Such a one
Am I to feare, or none.

Enter young Seyward.

  Y Sey. What is thy name?
  Macb. Thou'lt be affraid to heare it.
  Y Sey. No: though thou call'st thy selfe a hoter name
Then any is in hell.
  Macb. My name's *Macbeth.*
  Y Sey. The divell himselfe could not pronounce a Title
More hatefull to mine eare.
  Macb. No: nor more fearefull.
  Y Sey. Thou lyest abhorred Tyrant, with my Sword
Ile prove the lye thou speak st.

Fight, and young Seyward slaine.

  Macb. Thou was't borne of woman;
But Swords I smile at, Weapons laugh to scorne,
Brandish'd by man that's of a Woman borne.   *Exit.*

Alarums.   Enter Macduffe.

  Macd. That way the noise is: Tyrant shew thy face,
If thou beest slaine, and with no stroake of mine,
My Wife and Childrens Ghosts will haunt me still:
I cannot strike at wretched Kernes, whose armes

Are hyr'd to beare their Staves; either thou *Macbeth*,
Or else my Sword with an unbattered edge
I sheath againe undeeded. There thou should'st be,
By this great clatter, one of greatest note
Seemes bruited. Let me finde him Fortune,
And more I begge not.   *Exit.*   *Alarums.*

Enter Malcolme and Seyward.

Sey. This way my Lord, the Castles gently rendred:
The Tyrants people, on both sides do fight,
The Noble Thanes do bravely in the Warre,
The day almost it selfe professes yours,
And little is to do.
     Malc. We have met with Foes
That strike beside us.
     Sey. Enter Sir, the Castle.   *Exeunt.*   *Alarum*

Enter Macbeth.

Macb. Why should I play the Roman Foole, and dye
On mine owne sword? whiles I see lives, the gashes
Do better upon them.

Enter Macduffe.

     Macd. Turne Hell-hound, turne.
     Macb. Of all men else I have avoyded thee:
But get thee backe, my soule is too much charg'd
With blood of thine already.
     Macd. I have no words,
My voice is in my Sword, thou bloodier Villaine
Then tearmes can give thee out.   *Fight: Alarum*
     Macb. Thou loosest labour
As easie may'st thou the intrenchant Ayre
With thy keene Sword impresse, as make me bleed:
Let fall thy blade on vulnerable Crests,
I beare a charmed Life, which must not yeeld
To one of woman borne.
     Macd. Dispaire thy Charme,

And let the Angell whom thou still hast serv'd
Tell thee, *Macduffe* was from his Mothers womb
Untimely ript.

   Macb. Accursed be that tongue that tels mee so;
For it hath Cow'd my better part of man:
And be these Jugling Fiends no more beleev'd,
That palter with us in a double sence,
That keepe the word of promise to our eare,
And breake it to our hope. Ile not fight with thee.

   Macd. Then yeeld thee Coward,
And live to be the shew, and gaze o'th'time.
Wee'l have thee, as our rarer Monsters are
Painted upon a pole, and under-writ,
Heere may you see the Tyrant.

   Macb. I will not yeeld
To kisse the ground before young *Malcolmes* feet,
And to be baited with the Rabbles curse.
Though Byrnane wood be come to Dunsinane,
And thou oppos'd, being of no woman borne,
Yet I will try the last. Before my body,
I throw my warlike Shield: Lay on *Macduffe*,
And damn'd be him, that first cries hold, enough.

                Exeunt fighting.   *Alarums.*

Enter Fighting, and Macbeth slaine.

*Retreat, and Flourish. Enter with Drumme and Colours,
Malcolm, Seyward, Rosse, Thanes, & Soldiers.*

   Mal. I would the Friends we misse, were safe arriv'd.
   Sey. Some must go off: and yet by these I see,
So great a day as this is cheapely bought.
   Mal. *Macduffe* is missing, and your Noble Sonne.
   Rosse. Your son my Lord, ha's paid a souldiers debt,
He onely liv'd but till he was a man,
The which no sooner had his Prowesse confirm'd
In the unshrinking station where he fought,
But like a man he dy'de.

Sey. Then he is dead?

Rosse. I, and brought off the field: your cause of sorrow
Must not be measur'd by his worth, for then
It hath no end.

Sey. Had he his hurts before?

Rosse. I, on the Front.

Sey. Why then, Gods Soldier be he:
Had I as many Sonnes, as I have haires,
I would not wish them to a fairer death:
And so his Knell is knoll'd.

Mal. Hee's worth more sorrow,
And that Ile spend for him.

Sey. He's worth no more,
They say he parted well, and paid his score,
And so God be with him. Here comes newer comfort.

Enter Macduffe, with Macbeths head.

Macd. Haile King, for so thou art.
Behold where stands
Th'Usurpers cursed head: the time is free:
I see thee compast with thy Kingdomes Pearle,
That speake my salutation in their minds:
Whose voyces I desire alowd with mine.
Haile King of Scotland.

All. Haile King of Scotland.   *Flourish.*

Mal. We shall not spend a large expence of time,
Before we reckon with your severall loves,
And make us even with you. My Thanes and Kinsmen
Henceforth be Earles, the first that ever Scotland
In such an Honor nam'd: What's more to do,
Which would be planted newly with the time,
As calling home our exil'd Friends abroad,
That fled the Snares of watchfull Tyranny,
Producing forth the cruell Ministers
Of this dead Butcher, and his Fiend-like Queene;
Who (as 'tis thought) by selfe and violent hands,
Tooke off her life. This, and what needfull else

That call's upon us, by the Grace of Grace,
We will performe in measure, time, and place:
So thankes to all at once, and to each one,
Whom we invite, to see us Crown'd at Scone.

     Flourish   *Exeunt Omnes.*

       FINIS

Endnotes

Page 33
Gray-Malkin: a grey cat, a witch's familiar spirit; malkin also means a loose woman.

Padock: a toad.

All. Padock calls . . . : later editions often give this speech to one or other of the witches rather than all three.

Page 34
Serjeant: the equivalent of a Captain.

Kernes: Irish foot soldiers.

Gallowgrosses: Irish armoured infantrymen.

damned Quarry: changed by Johnson, Malone, etc. to 'damned quarrel'; however, F1's reading can stand in the light of the play's presentation of Macbeth as the quarry of fortune.

Shew'd like a Rebells Whore: while she smiled on him she deceived him.

Disdayning Fortune: because fortune dallied with the rebels Macbeth disdained her, and conquered instead as the minion or servant of valour.

Nave: navel.

Cousin: both Macbeth and Duncan were grandsons of King Malcolm of Scotland.

Banquho: this spelling is that found in Raphael Holinshed's *Chronicles of England, Scotland, and Ireland*. It is spelled 'Banquoh' when it first appears in the text, suggesting that the compositor may have reversed the last two letters. At its next and in all subsequent apearances it is spelt without the terminal 'h' in the form in which it appears in later editions.

Page 35
Thane: from the Anglo-Saxon *thegen*, literally a servant, technically in this sense it means a King's servant although they were feudal authorities themselves.

[105]

Endnotes

a haste: *a* is removed in F2.

Saint Colmes ynch: Inchcolm is the Island of St Columba in the Firth of Forth. Its name is changed to Colmes-hill in F2–4, while Pope took the line to refer to the Hebridean island of Iona, also associated with St Columba.

Dollars: this term is anachronistic in the play since the dollar (thaler) was not coined until 1518.

Page 36

mouncht: to chew with closed lips from the French *manger*.

Aroynt: this word appears to be a Shakespearean coinage, first used in *Macbeth* and in *King Lear* (1605), in F3–4 it is changed to anoint.

rumpe-fed: an allusion to her poverty, suggesting she is fed on the rump or poor ends of meat.

Ronyon: mangy, scabby.

Aleppo . . . Tiger: Richard Hakluyt's *The Principal Voyages, Navigations, Traffics and Discoveries of the English Nation* (1589 and 1598–60) print accounts of a voyage to Aleppo in 1583 by a ship of this name.

Syve: Thomas Scott's *Discovery of Witchcraft* (1584) talks of witches being able to go to sea in eggshells; this might be Shakespeare's inspiration for this image.

Card: map, from French *carte*.

Page 37

weyward: perverse, subsequently spelt *weird*.

Soris: apparently meant to refer to Duncan's camp at Forres; this appears to be a misreading by the compositor.

Noble having: that which he already has, as opposed to his expectation, is noble.

Page 38

Sinell: Macbeth's father.

insane Root: hemlock, the eating of which caused insanity.

silenc'd with that: the King is dumbstruck with admiration.

Page 39

Can post with post: presumably an error for *Came post with post*, that is with each successive bringer of news.

Endnotes

Onely: omitted by some editions as redundant.

harrold: changed to herrald in F2–3 and herald in F4 *et seq*.

Page 40

unfix my Heire: Rowe *et seq* make this read *Hair*, although a quibble may be intended here as in Siward's '*Had I as many Sonnes, and I have haires*' in Act 5, Scene 7.

strange Garments: new garments, here signifying new honours.

favour : indulgence.

The Interim having weigh'd it: i.e. when we have had time to consider.

Page 41

those in Commission: i.e. those commissioned to supervise the execution.

proportion: that thanks and payment would be in proportion to what you deserve.

Page 42

Wanton: unrestrained.

Herbenger: one who prepares lodgings.

Page 43

Missives: messages.

Milke of humane kindnesse: the quality of humanity.

the Golden Round: crown.

Metaphysicall: supernatural.

Page 44

Raven: traditionally a bird of ill-omen.

mortall thoughts: deadly thoughts.

Page 45

The Temple-haunting Barlet: Nicholas Rowe corrected this to Martlet, the house-martin.

God-eyld: compositor's error for Go-yield.

Page 46

Ermites: hermits; Lady Macbeth is suggesting that they will be indebted to Duncan like hermits supported by his charity.

Purveyor: provider or harbinger.

Endnotes

Sewer: chief servant who directed the placing of dishes on the table.

surcease: from the Old French *sursis*, meaning to stop or stay a legal proceeding.

Banke and Schoole of time: Theobald's emendation Shoal is generally adopted here, especially as Schoole is an early alternative spelling for Shoal, but F's 'School' can stand if the allusion is taken to be to gambling rather than to rivers. This suggestion was made by A.P. Reimer in a note in *Sydney Studies in English*, vol. 5 (1979–80), pp. 96–101.

Page 47

sightlesse Curriors: the winds.

the poore Cat i'th'Addage: the addage referred to appears to be that recorded in John Heywood's Epigrams (collected in *John Heywood's Woorkes* (1562)): 'The cat that would eat fish but would not wet its feet.'

Page 48

convince: overpower, from the Latin *convinco*, to overcome or conquer.

Lymbeck: an alembic or retort.

spungie: drunken.

Page 51

Tarquins ravishing sides: Sextus Tarquinius, son of King Tarquin of Rome, raped Lucrece, the virtuous wife of Collatinus; her fate so enrages the people of Rome that they exile the Tarquins and establish a republic. His story provides the background for Shakespeare's early poem *The Rape of Lucrece* (1594). Since Pope's edition of *Macbeth* strides has been substituted, although sides, suggesting sideling, could be used.

sowre and firme-set Earth: Pope's conjecture of 'sure' for 'sowre' makes sense in conjunction with *firme-set*. In his own edition Pope thought the word intended was 'sound'.

Bell-man: night watchman.

mock their charge: abandon their duties.

Possets: a night-time drink made from hot milk poured over ale or wine, with sugar and eggs boiled in it.

Page 52

ravel'd Sleeve of Care: a ravelled sleeve is one frayed or worn; Edmond Malone suggested that what was being referred to was 'sleave', a type of tangled silk, and some later editions, such as the Cambridge edition of 1892, adopt this spelling and meaning.

unbend your Noble strength: relax.

Endnotes

Page 53

Ile guild the Faces of the Groomes withall: she will cover their faces with blood as one might gild a painting or statue with gold, also entailed is a pun on guilt/gilt in the following line.

incarnadine: to make blood-red.

your Constancie/Hath left you unattended: your firmness of purpose has abandoned you.

Page 54

Equivocator: a juggler with the truth; this is possibly a topical allusion to the Jesuit priest Garnet, tried in March 1606 for his role in the Gunpowder Conspiracy.

English Taylor . . . French Hose: tailors were proverbially accused of skimping on cloth, something easy to do with the style of French hose (which were either long and baggy or short and tight).

Page 55

gave thee the Lye: meaning both tricked him and made him lie down.

cast him: either threw off the effects of the wine, or vomited up the wine.

I have almost slipt the houre: let the hour slip by.

The labour we delight in, Physicks paine: the work I enjoy purges pain.

limitted service: appointed duty.

Page 56

Master-peece: greatest work.

Gorgon: a mythical figure who turned to stone all who looked on her.

Deaths counterfeit: sleep is the image or imitation of death.

countenance: behold or confront.

Page 57

Lees: dregs.

expedition: prompt or hasty action.

pawser: one who stops to consider.

Page 58

breech'd: covered as a body is with trousers.

That most may clayme this argument for ours: who are most involved in the subject.

Endnotes

augure hole: a small hole made with an auger, that is, a small boring tool, here possibly a dagger.

Our tears are not yet brewed: not ready to pour.

undivulg'd pretence: hidden purpose.

Page 59
daintie: particular.

Hath trifled former knowings: made previous experience insignifcant.

Page 60
Gods benyson: God's blessing.

Page 61
Senit: a brief trumpet call.

Lady Lenox: a comma is missing here, the *Lady* is Lady Macbeth.

all-thing unbecomming: altogether or totally unbecoming.

cause of State: affairs of state.

Page 62
While then: until then.

To be thus, is nothing . . . . : to be King, is nothing unless secure in the position.

Gripe: grasp.

fil'd: defiled.

eternall Jewell: soul.

Page 63
Lyst: the tilt-yard, scene of tournaments.

th'utterance: the uttermost.

Past in probation with you: reviewed or considered with you.

borne in hand: deceived.

halfe a Soule: a half-wit.

Notion: mind.

Showghes, Water-Rugs and Demy-Wolves: breeds of dogs, the first two characterised by their shaggy coats, the third a cross between a wolf and a dog.

Endnotes

clipt: called.

valued file: list of qualities.

Page 64

distance: quarrell, from the Old French term *destance*.

neer'st of Life: what most concerns my life.

avouch: justify.

Page 65

Spy o'th'time: place to watch from at the time of the ambush.

something: somewhat, at a distance.

cleareness: an alibi.

scorch'd the Snake: slashed it, as with a knife.

Page 66

apply to Banquo: be given to Banquo.

shard-borne: born on a dung-heap or carried (borne) on scaly wings.

Page 67

seeling: blinding; the term is taken from falconry where falcons eyelids were often sown together to make the bird manageable.

Offices: duties.

To the direction just: just as the directions were given.

within the note of expectation: the list of expected guests.

Page 68

her State: her place of eminence.

Page 69

Non-pareill: paragon.

founded: immovable.

trenched: cut.

vouch'd: warranted.

Page 70

upon a thought: in a moment.

Ayre-drawne-Dagger: drawn in or through the air.

Endnotes

mortall murthers: fatal wounds.

And all to all: good wishes to all.

Page 72
admir'd: wondered at.

Augures: auguries.

Maggot Pyes, & Choughes: magpies and a bird of the rook family.

Page 73
All causes shall give way: all else will take second place.

self-abuse: self-delusion.

initiate fear: a novice's fear.

Beldams: hags.

close: secret.

Acheron: a river in Hell.

dismall: disastrous.

Page 74
Artificiall: artful.

Security: overconfidence.

hit: agreed with.

borne: conducted.

Page 75
broad: plainspoken.

Sonnes of Duncan: this appears to be an error in F, as Donalbain went to Ireland and does not feature again in the play. F2–4 changed lives, two lines later, to live to make it agree with Sonnes.

Edward: Edward the Confessor, King of England.

absolute : peremptory or curt.

clogges: obstructs.

Page 76
brinded: brindled.

Hedge-Pigge: the hedgehog; Brooke suggests that the female hedgehog is meant.

Endnotes

Harpier: the third witch's familiar, possibly a Harpy.

Sweltred: sweated.

Fenny: muddy, or possibly, fen-dwelling.

Howlet: small owl.

Maw: dried flesh.

Gulfe: stomach parts.

ravin'd: glutted.

Ditch-deliver'd: delivered in secret and therefore unbaptised.

slab: another term for thick; there are numerous similar cases in F *Macbeth* of tautologous phrases, e.g. *access and passage* in Lady Macbeth's soliloquy.

Chawdron: entrails.

Page 77
yesty: yeasty, frothing.

Navigation: shipping.

Germaine: seeds.

Page 78
harp'd: given voice, as from song, accompanied by a harp.

Page 79
Great Byrnam Wood, to high Dunsmane: F's spelling of both of these locations varies: this particular spelling of Dunsinane may result from a misreading that joins the 'i' to the medial 'n'.

impresse: enlist, against the will, for military service; Angus in Act 5, Scene 2 suggests that this is the state of Macbeth's army in the final conflict.

boadments: predictions.

mortall Custome: death .

two fold Balles and treble Scepters: a reference is being made here to King James who unified the kingdoms of England and Scotland: Scottish kings were invested with one sceptre and one orb and English kings with two sceptres and one orb.

Blood-bolter'd: clotted with blood.

Page 80
Antique: antic, grotesque or fantastic. .

Endnotes

firstlings: first born, here meaning first thoughts without further consideration.

Page 81

diminitive: a variant of diminutive.

fits o'th'Season: disorders of the times.

Page 82

disgrace: either caused by his weeping at her condition, by gossip at his presence during her husband's absence, or by implicating him in Macduff's treason.

Lime: bird-lime, a form of glue painted on to trees to catch birds.

Gin: snare.

Thou speak'st withall thy wit: you speak with all the little wit you have but it is still very shrewd.

Page 84

Bestride our downfall Birthdome: stand protectively over our fallen country.

You may discerne of him: editors to the end of the nineteenth century tended to follow Theobald's emendation of 'discerne' to 'deserve'; however, in the light of Malcolm's caution, F's *discerne* can stand as meaning, 'You may see something to your advantage by betraying me.'

Nature may recoyle/In an Imperiall charge: kingship or royal command may alter nature.

Jealousies: suspicions.

Page 85

The Title, is affear'd: there are two possible meanings depending on whether F's spelling is accepted. Hanmer altered the spelling, and thus the word, to 'afeered', a legal term meaning confirmed: the meaning of the line thus becomes 'Macbeth's title is confirmed by Malcolm's unwillingness to resist'. If F's spelling is retained the line can also be read as saying that Malcolm is afraid to press his title against Macbeth.

sundry wayes: different ways.

Cesterne: a cistern, a large tank.

continent Impediments: obstructions caused by continence or restraint.

Page 86

Convey: carry on secretly.

stanchlesse: unstopped.

Endnotes

Quarrels: perhaps, literally, arrowheads, but also, more generally, contention.

Foysons: resources.

Of your meere Owne: belonging to you.

All these are portable: all these [faults] can be borne.

rellish of: taste for.

Page 87

Uprore: throw into confusion.

By his owne Interdiction stands accust: F2 changed 'acust' to 'accurst'; another possible reading, closer to F's spelling, is 'acus'd', especially given the legal sense of interdiction.

traines: tricks.

modest Wisedome: caution.

they heere approach: they is presumably an error for thy, the meaning of the line being: before thy coming here.

Page 88

at a point: prepared.

convinces: conquers.

assay of Art: efforts of medical skill.

Page 91

This time goes manly: either, at this time we are ready to act, or, the rythm of these remarks is manly and warlike.

perturbation: disorder.

Page 92

stand close: stand concealed.

Page 93

sorely charg'd : heavily burdened.

dignity: value.

Page 94

unruffe youths: beardless young men.

Protest: proclaim.

Faith-breach: treason.

Endnotes

Med'cine: i.e. Malcolm.

Page 95
sway: rule.

Patch: a fool or a clown.

cheere me ever, or dis-eate me now: if cheere is taken to refer to chair then the line means, the success of this engagement will determine whether I am enthroned hereafter or dethroned at once.

Seare: withered state.

Page 96
moe: more.

skirre: scour.

cast/The Water of my Land: examine it as a physician would examine the urine of a patient.

Cyme: some form of purgative drug is meant here, either senna or thyme, sium (wild parsley), cumin or Ocyme (basil).

Page 97
shadow: conceal.

stroakes must arbitrate: only battle will decide.

Page 98
forc'd: either reinforced or, possibly, stuffed.

darefull: bold, full of daring.

Fell of haire: hair on the skin.

Page 99
wracke: disaster.

Battell: one of the divisions of the army.

Page 100
Beare-like: like a bear tied to a stake to be baited by dogs.

Page 101
strike beside us: deliberately miss us when they strike.

play the Roman Foole: commit suicide in defeat.

Appendix

THE TRAGEDIE OF
MACBETH.

Actus Primus. Scœna Prima.

Thunder and Lightning. Enter three Witches.

1. Hen shall we three meet againe?
In Thunder, Lightning, or in Raine?
   2. When the Hurley-burley's done,
When the Battaile's lost, and wonne.
   3. That will be ere the set of Sunne.
   1. Where the place?
2. Vpon the Heath.
3. There to meet with *Macbeth*.
1. I come, *Gray-Malkin*.
All. Padock calls anon: faire is foule, and foule is faire,
Houer through the fogge and filthie ayre.   *Exeunt.*

Scena Secunda.

Alarum within. Enter King Malcome, Donalbaine, Lenox, with attendants, meeting a bleeding Captaine.

King. What bloody man is that? he can report,
As seemeth by his plight, of the Reuolt
The newest state.
   Mal. This is the Serieant,
Who like a good and hardie Souldier fought
'Gainst my Captiuitie: Haile braue friend;
Say to the King, the knowledge of the Broyle,
As thou didst leaue it.
   Cap. Doubtfull it stood,
As two spent Swimmers, that doe cling together,
And choake their Art: The mercilesse *Macdonwald*
(Worthie to be a Rebell, for to that
The multiplying Villanies of Nature
Doe swarme vpon him) from the Westerne Isles
Of Kernes and Gallowgrosses is supply'd,
And Fortune on his damned Quarry smiling,
Shew'd like a Rebells Whore: but all's too weake:
For braue *Macbeth* (well hee deserues that Name)
Disdayning Fortune, with his brandisht Steele,
Which smoak'd with bloody execution
(Like Valours Minion) caru'd out his passage,
Till hee fac'd the Slaue:
Which neu'r shooke hands, nor bad farwell to him,
Till he vnseam'd him from the Naue toth' Chops,
And fix'd his Head vpon our Battlements.

King. O valiant Cousin, worthy Gentleman.
   Cap. As whence the Sunne 'gins his reflection,
Shipwracking Stormes, and direfull Thunders:
So from that Spring, whence comfort seem'd to come,
Discomfort swells: Marke King of Scotland, marke,
No sooner Iustice had, with Valour arm'd,
Compell'd these skipping Kernes to trust their heeles,
But the Norweyan Lord, surueying vantage,
With furbusht Armes, and new supplyes of men,
Began a fresh assault.
   King. Dismay'd not this our Captaines, *Macbeth* and *Banquoh*?
   Cap. Yes, as Sparrowes, Eagles;
Or the Hare, the Lyon:
If I say sooth, I must report they were
As Cannons ouer-charg'd with double Cracks,
So they doubly redoubled stroakes vpon the Foe:
Except they meant to bathe in reeking Wounds,
Or memorize another *Golgotha*,
I cannot tell: but I am faint,
My Gashes cry for helpe.
   King. So well thy words become thee, as thy wounds,
They smack of Honor both: Goe get him Surgeons.

Enter Rosse and Angus.

Who comes here?
   Mal. The worthy Thane of Rosse.
   Lenox. What a haste lookes through his eyes?
So should he looke, that seemes to speake things strange.
   Rosse. God saue the King.
   King. Whence cam'st thou, worthy *Thane?*
   Rosse. From Fiffe, great King,
Where the Norweyan Banners flowt the Skie,
And fanne our people cold.
Norway himselfe, with terrible numbers,
Assisted by that most disloyall Traytor,
The *Thane* of Cawdor, began a dismall Conflict,
Till that *Bellona's* Bridegroome, lapt in proofe,
Confronted him with selfe-comparisons,
Point against Point, rebellious Arme 'gainst Arme,
Curbing his lauish spirit: and to conclude,
The Victorie fell on vs.
   King. Great happinesse.
   Rosse. That now, *Sweno*, the Norwayes King,
Craues composition:
Nor would we deigne him buriall of his men,
Till he disbursed, at Saint *Colmes* ynch,
Ten thousand Dollars, to our generall vse.
                                    King: No

King. No more that *Thane* of Cawdor shall deceiue
Our Bosome interest : Goe pronounce his present death,
And with his former Title greet *Macbeth.*
Rosse. Ile see it done.
King. What he hath lost, Noble *Macbeth* hath wonne.

Exeunt.

Scena Tertia.

Thunder. Enter the three Witches.

1. Where hast thou beene, Sister ?
2. Killing Swine.
3. Sister, where thou ?
1. A Saylors Wife had Chestnuts in her Lappe,
And mouncht, & mouncht, and mouncht :
Giue me, quoth I.
Aroynt thee, Witch, the rumpe-fed Ronyon cryes.
Her Husband's to Aleppo gone, Master o'th' *Tiger* :
But in a Syue Ile thither sayle,
And like a Rat without a tayle,
Ile doe, Ile doe, and Ile doe.
 2. Ile giue thee a Winde.
 1. Th'art kinde.
 3. And I another.
1. I my selfe haue all the other,
And the very Ports they blow,
All the Quarters that they know,
I'th' Ship-mans Card.
Ile dreyne him drie as Hay :
Sleepe shall neyther Night nor Day
Hang vpon his Pent-house Lid :
He shall liue a man forbid :
Wearie Seu'nights, nine times nine,
Shall he dwindle, peake, and pine :
Though his Barke cannot be lost,
Yet it shall be Tempest-tost.
Looke what I haue.
 2. Shew me, shew me.
 1. Here I haue a Pilots Thumbe,
Wrackt, as homeward he did come.   *Drum within.*
 3. A Drumme, a Drumme :
Macbeth doth come.
All. The weyward Sisters, hand in hand,
Posters of the Sea and Land,
Thus doe goe, about, about,
Thrice to thine, and thrice to mine,
And thrice againe, to make vp nine.
Peace, the Charme's wound vp.

Enter Macbeth and Banquo.

Macb. So foule and faire a day I haue not seene.
Banquo. How farre is't call'd to Soris ? What are these,
So wither'd, and so wilde in their attyre,
That looke not like th'Inhabitants o'th'Earth,
And yet are on't ? Liue you, or are you aught
That man may question ? you seeme to vnderstand me,
By each at once her choppie finger laying
Vpon her skinnie Lips : you should be Women,
And yet your Beards forbid me to interprete
That you are so.

Mac. Speake if you can : what are you ?
1. All haile *Macbeth*, haile to thee *Thane* of Glamis.
2. All haile *Macbeth*, haile to thee *Thane* of Cawdor.
3. All haile *Macbeth*, that shalt be King hereafter.
Banq. Good Sir, why doe you start, and seeme to feare
Things that doe sound so faire ? i'th'name of truth
Are ye fantasticall, or that indeed
Which outwardly ye shew ? My Noble Partner
You greet with present Grace, and great prediction
Of Noble hauing, and of Royall hope,
That he seemes wrapt withall : to me you speake not.
If you can looke into the Seedes of Time,
And say, which Graine will grow, and which will not,
Speake then to me, who neyther begge, nor feare
Your fauors, nor your hate.
1. Hayle.
2. Hayle.
3. Hayle.
1. Lesser then *Macbeth*, and greater.
2. Not so happy, yet much happyer.
3. Thou shalt get Kings, though thou be none :
So all haile *Macbeth*, and *Banquo.*
1. *Banquo*, and *Macbeth*, all haile.
Macb. Stay you imperfect Speakers, tell me more. :
By *Sinells* death, I know I am *Thane* of Glamis,
But how, of Cawdor ? the *Thane* of Cawdor liues
A prosperous Gentleman : And to be King,
Stands not within the prospect of beleefe,
No more then to be Cawdor. Say from whence
You owe this strange Intelligence, or why
Vpon this blasted Heath you stop our way
With such Prophetique greeting :
Speake, I charge you.   *Witches vanish.*
Banq. The Earth hath bubbles, as the Water ha's,
And these are of them : whither are they vanish'd ?
Macb. Into the Ayre : and what seem'd corporall,
Melted, as breath into the Winde.
Would they had stay'd.
Banq. Were such things here, as we doe speake about ?
Or haue we eaten on the insane Root,
That takes the Reason Prisoner ?
Macb. Your Children shall be Kings.
Banq. You shall be King.
Macb. And *Thane* of Cawdor too : went it not so ?
Banq. Toth' selfe-same tune, and words : who's here ?

Enter Rosse and Angus.

Rosse. The King hath happily receiu'd, *Macbeth*,
The newes of thy successe : and when he reades
Thy personall Venture in the Rebels fight,
His Wonders and his Prayses doe contend,
Which should be thine, or his : silenc'd with that,
In viewing o're the rest o'th'selfe-same day,
He findes thee in the stout Norweyan Rankes,
Nothing afeard of what thy selfe didst make
Strange Images of death, as thick as Tale
Can post with post, and euery one did beare
Thy prayses in his Kingdomes great defence,
And powr'd them downe before him.
Ang. Wee are sent,
To giue thee from our Royall Master thanks,
Onely to harrold thee into his sight,
Not pay thee.
Rosse. And for an earnest of a greater Honor,
He bad me, from him, call thee *Thane* of Cawdor

In

In which addition,haile most worthy *Thane*,
For it is thine.

Banq. What, can the Deuill speake true?

Macb. The *Thane* of Cawdor liues:
Why doe you dresse me in borrowed Robes?

Ang. Who was the *Thane*, liues yet,
But vnder heauie Iudgement beares that Life,
Which he deserues to loose.
Whether he was combin'd with those of Norway,
Or did lyne the Rebell with hidden helpe,
And vantage ; or that with both he labour'd
In his Countreyes wracke, I know not :
But Treasons Capitall,confess'd,and prou'd,
Haue ouerthrowne him.

Macb. Glamys,and *Thane* of Cawdor:
The greatest is behinde. Thankes for your paines.
Doe you not hope your Children shall be Kings,
When those that gaue the *Thane* of Cawdor to me,
Promis'd no lesse to them.

Banq. That trusted home,
Might yet enkindle you vnto the Crowne,
Besides the *Thane* of Cawdor. But 'tis strange :
And oftentimes,to winne vs to our harme,
The Instruments of Darknesse tell vs Truths,
Winne vs with honest Trifles,to betray's
In deepest consequence.
Cousins, a word, I pray you.

Macb. Two Truths are told,
As happy Prologues to the swelling Act
Of the Imperiall Theame. I thanke you Gentlemen :
This supernaturall solliciting
Cannot be ill ; cannot be good.
If ill ? why hath it giuen me earnest of successe,
Commencing in a Truth ? I am *Thane* of Cawdor.
If good ? why doe I yeeld to that suggestion,
Whose horrid Image doth vnfixe my Heire,
And make my seated Heart knock at my Ribbes,
Against the vse of Nature ? Present Feares
Are lesse then horrible Imaginings :
My Thought, whose Murther yet is but fantasticall,
Shakes so my single state of Man,
That Function is smother'd in surmise,
And nothing is,but what is not.

Banq. Looke how our Partner's rapt.

Macb. If Chance will haue me King,
Why Chance may Crowne me,
Without my stirre.

Banq. New Honors come vpon him
Like our strange Garments,cleaue not to their mould,
But with the aid of vse.

Macb. Come what come may,
Time,and the Houre,runs through the roughest Day.

Banq. Worthy *Macbeth*, wee stay vpon your leysure.

Macb. Giue me your fauour :
My dull Braine was wrought with things forgotten.
Kinde Gentlemen,your paines are registred,
Where euery day I turne the Leafe,
To reade them.
Let vs toward the King : thinke vpon
What hath chanc'd : and at more time,
The *Interim* hauing weigh'd it,let vs speake
Our free Hearts each to other.

Banq. Very gladly.

Macb. Till then enough :
Come friends.   *Exeunt.*

Scena Quarta.

Flourish. Enter King,Lenox, Malcolme,
Donalbaine, and Attendants.

King. Is execution done on *Cawdor* ?
Or not those in Commission yet return'd ?

Mal. My Liege,they are not yet come backe.
But I haue spoke with one that saw him die :
Who did report,that very franckly hee
Confess'd his Treasons,implor'd your Highnesse Pardon,
And set forth a deepe Repentance :
Nothing in his Life became him,
Like the leauing it. Hee dy'de,
As one that had beene studied in his death,
To throw away the dearest thing he ow'd.
As 'twere a carelesse Trifle.

King. There's no Art,
To finde the Mindes construction in the Face :
He was a Gentleman,on whom I built
An absolute Trust.

Enter Macbeth,Banquo,Rosse,and Angus.

O worthyest Cousin,
The sinne of my Ingratitude euen now
Was heauie on me. Thou art so farre before,
That swiftest Wing of Recompence is slow,
To ouertake thee. Would thou hadst lesse deseru'd
That the proportion both of thanks,and payment,
Might haue beene mine : onely I haue left to say,
More is thy due,then more then all can pay.

Macb. The seruice,and the loyaltie I owe,
In doing it,payes it selfe.
Your Highnesse part,is to receiue our Duties :
And our Duties are to your Throne,and State,
Children,and Seruants ; which doe but what they should,
By doing euery thing safe toward your Loue
And Honor.

King. Welcome hither :
I haue begun to plant thee,and will labour
To make thee full of growing. Noble *Banquo*,
That hast no lesse deseru'd,nor must be knowne
No lesse to haue done so : Let me enfold thee,
And hold thee to my Heart.

Banq. There if I grow,
The Haruest is your owne.

King. My plenteous Ioyes,
Wanton in fulnesse,seeke to hide themselues
In drops of sorrow. Sonnes,Kinsmen, *Thanes*,
And you whose places are the nearest,know,
We will establish our Estate vpon
Our eldest, *Malcolme*,whom we name hereafter,
The Prince of Cumberland : which Honor must
Not vnaccompanied,inuest him onely,
But signes of Noblenesse,like Starres,shall shine
On all deseruers. From hence to *Envernes*,
And binde vs further to you.

Macb. The Rest is Labor, which is not vs'd for you :
Ile be my selfe the Herbenger,and make ioyfull
The hearing of my Wife,with your approach :
So humbly take my leaue.

King. My worthy *Cawdor*.

Macb. The Prince of Cumberland : that is a step,
On which I must fall downe,or else o're-leape,

m m   For

For in my way it lyes. Starres hide your fires,
Let not Light see my black and deepe desires:
The Eye winke at the Hand; yet let that bee,
Which the Eye feares, when it is done to see.   *Exit.*

King. True, worthy *Banquo*: he is full so valiant,
And in his commendations, I am fed:
It is a Banquet to me. Let's after him,
Whose care is gone before, to bid vs welcome:
It is a peerelesse Kinsman.   *Flourish. Exeunt.*

Scena Quinta.

Enter Macbeths Wife alone with a Letter.

Lady. They met me in the day of successe: and I haue
learn'd by the perfect'st report, they haue more in them, then
mortall knowledge. When I burnt in desire to question them
further, they made themselues Ayre, into which they vanish'd.
Whiles I stood rapt in the wonder of it, came Missiues from
the King, who all-hail'd me Thane of Cawdor, by which Title
before, these weyward Sisters saluted me, and referr'd me to
the comming on of time, with haile King that shalt be. This
haue I thought good to deliuer thee (my dearest Partner of
Greatnesse) that thou might'st not loose the dues of reioycing
by being ignorant of what Greatnesse is promis'd thee. Lay
it to thy heart, and farewell.

Glamys thou art, and Cawdor, and shalt be
What thou art promis'd: yet doe I feare thy Nature,
It is too full o'th' Milke, of humane kindnesse,
To catch the neerest way. Thou would'st be great,
Art not without Ambition, but without
The illnesse should attend it. What thou would'st highly,
That would'st thou holily: would'st not play-false,
And yet would'st wrongly winne.
Thould'st haue, great Glamys, that which cryes,
Thus thou must doe, if thou haue it;
And that which rather thou do'st feare to doe,
Then wishest should be vndone. High thee hither,
That I may powre my Spirits in thine Eare,
And chastise with the valour of my Tongue
All that impedies thee from the Golden Round,
Which Fate and Metaphysicall ayde doth seeme
To haue thee crown'd withall.   *Enter Messenger.*
What is your tidings?

Mess. The King comes here to Night.
Lady. Thou'rt mad to say it.
Is not thy Master with him? who, wer't so,
Would haue inform'd for preparation.

Mess. So please you, it is true: our *Thane* is comming:
One of my fellowes had the speed of him;
Who almost dead for breath, had scarcely more
Then would make vp his Message.

Lady. Giue him tending,
He brings great newes.   *Exit Messenger.*
The Rauen himselfe is hoarse,
That croakes the fatall entrance of *Duncan*
Vnder my Battlements. Come you Spirits,
That tend on mortall thoughts, vnsex me here,
And fill me from the Crowne to the Toe, top-full
Of direst Crueltie: make thick my blood,
Stop vp th'accesse, and passage to Remorse,
That no compunctious visitings of Nature

Shake my fell purpose, nor keepe peace betweene
Th'effect, and hit. Come to my Womans Brests,
And take my Milke for Gall, you murth'ring Ministers,
Where-euer, in your sightlesse substances,
You wait on Natures Mischiefe. Come thick Night,
And pall thee in the dunnest smoake of Hell,
That my keene Knife see not the Wound it makes,
Not Heauen peepe through the Blanket of the darke,
To cry, hold, hold.   *Enter Macbeth.*
Great Glamys, worthy Cawdor,
Greater then both, by the all-haile hereafter,
Thy Letters haue transported me beyond
This ignorant present, and I feele now
The future in the instant.

Macb. My dearest Loue,
Duncan comes here to Night.
Lady. And when goes hence?
Macb. To morrow, as he purposes.
Lady. O neuer,
Shall Sunne that Morrow see.
Your Face, my Thane, is as a Booke, where men
May reade strange matters, to beguile the time.
Looke like the time, beare welcome in your Eye,
Your Hand, your Tongue: looke like th'innocent flower,
But be the Serpent vnder't. He that's comming,
Must be prouided for: and you shall put
This Nights great Businesse into my dispatch,
Which shall to all our Nights, and Dayes to come,
Giue solely soueraigne sway, and Masterdome.
Macb. We will speake further.
Lady. Onely looke vp cleare:
To alter fauor, euer is to feare:
Leaue all the rest to me.   *Exeunt.*

Scena Sexta.

Hoboyes, and Torches. Enter King, Malcolme,
Donalbaine, Banquo, Lenox, Macduff,
Rosse, Angus, and Attendants.

King. This Castle hath a pleasant seat,
The ayre nimbly and sweetly recommends it selfe
Vnto our gentle sences.

Banq. This Guest of Summer,
The Temple-haunting Barlet does approue,
By his loued Mansonry, that the Heauens breath
Smells wooingly here: no Iutty frieze,
Buttrice, nor Coigne of Vantage, but this Bird
Hath made his pendant Bed, and procreant Cradle,
Where they must breed, and haunt: I haue obseru'd
The ayre is delicate.   *Enter Lady.*

King. See, see, our honor'd Hostesse:
The Loue that followes vs, sometime is our trouble,
Which still we thanke as Loue. Herein I teach you,
How you shall bid God-eyld vs for your paines,
And thanke vs for your trouble.

Lady. All our seruice,
In euery point twice done, and then done double,
Were poore, and single Businesse to contend
Against those Honors deepe, and broad,
Wherewith your Maiestie loades our House:
For those of old, and the late Dignities,
Heap'd vp to them, we rest your Ermites.

                                King. Where's